THE PLAY OF PERSONALITY
IN THE RESTORATION THEATRE

Anthony Masters

THE PLAY OF PERSONALITY IN THE RESTORATION THEATRE

edited by Simon Trussler

THE BOYDELL PRESS

Copyright © Estate of Anthony Masters
1992

Text Editor: Simon Trussler
Picture Editor: Christopher Baugh

First published 1992 by The Boydell Press, Woodbridge

The Boydell Press is an imprint of Boydell & Brewer Ltd
PO Box 9, Woodbridge, Suffolk IP12 3DF, UK
and of Boydell & Brewer Inc.
PO Box 41026, Rochester, NY 14604, USA

ISBN 0 85115 326 7

British Library Cataloguing-in-Publication Data
A catalogue record for this book is available from the British Library

Library of Congress Cataloging-in-Publication Data applied for

This publication is printed on acid-free paper

Typeset in 11 on 13 point Palatino by
L. Anderson Typesetting
Woodchurch, Kent TN26 3TB
and printed in Great Britain
by The Five Castles Press, Ipswich

Contents

Illustrations

Acknowledgements

In addition to the many private owners and directors of galleries who have kindly given permission for illustrations to be reproduced in this book, and who are individually acknowledged in the captions to each item, my special thanks are due to my friends Roger Morsley Smith and Nicole Segre for their help, and also to Marianne Calmann, who first encouraged me to write this book.

I am also indebted to all the experts who have helped me while I was writing and researching this book, notably (and inevitably) Raymond Mander and Joe Mitchenson; Elspeth A. Evans of the National Portrait Gallery; F. N. Mason at Knole; John Sunderland, Witt Librarian at the Courtauld Institute of Art; Joan Pollard, Philippa Glanville, and Valerie Cumming at the Museum of London; the staff of the British Museum Print Room and the Mary Evans Picture Library; Katherine Hudson of the Mansell Collection; Janice Clement of the *TV Times*, and Owen Hale, Publicity Officer of the Thorndike Theatre, Leatherhead; Garth Hall and David Wright at the Victoria and Albert Museum, as well as the staff of the Theatre Collection; and Hilarie Faberman, Julian Badcock, Graham Reynolds, and Claude Blair for their help with Augustus Egg.

I am also most grateful to Sir John Gielgud, for an invaluable conversation about *Venice Preserv'd*; to John Christopher Marcus, for his help with Restoration astrology; and to Betty Shaw and Mary Morton, who directed me as a student in productions of Etherege and Congreve, and taught me so much about Restoration comedy technique.

The Author

Anthony Masters.

AT THE TIME of his sudden death on 3 January 1985, at the tragically early age of 36, Anthony Masters had for two years been deputy theatre critic of *The Times* — a free-lance position for which he had sacrificed the security of a staff appointment, and which should have been the start of a career on which he had long been determined.

Masters was academically brilliant: he was Senior Scholar at Winchester, and Scholar at King's College, Cambridge, where he took a first-class degree in Classics. But he never considered an academic career: his first love was for the theatre, and to it he brought all his wit, humour, and zest for life.

His other great enthusiasms, for travel and gastronomy, led him first into publishing, successively with Ernest Benn, working on the *Blue Guides*, and then with the Egon Ronay Organisation. When opportunity permitted, he joined *The Times*, working first in the letters department under Geoffrey Woolley — who encouraged the love of theatre that led Masters to keep copious private notes on the productions he saw, and then to take the decisive step of moving over to the arts pages.

In a very short period, the fairness and enthusiasm of Masters's reviews earned him great respect in the profession, as the obituary notice in *The Times* reflected at the time of his death:

Tony Masters's first notices . . . showed his fluent wit. He could have fallen into the trap of becoming the type of critic who builds a review around a series of witticisms. But his deep love of the theatre stifled that. Within a few months he was delivering judgements which were just, cleanly-phrased, and much respected.

Each comment passed was the result of careful research and the gathering of background information, plus the experience of a vast number of performances attended from childhood onwards. Probably his greatest quality was enthusiasm, vital to every newspaper critic. When he was angered by a production he said so in terms that were acerbic without being offensive; when he admired he wrote in a way to send his admirers rushing to the box office. . . . He will be greatly missed, both by The Times *and by theatres all over Britain.*

An Anthony Masters Memorial Scholarship to the Guildhall School of Music and Drama has subsequently been created, and there are plans for a further scholarship bearing his name, to King's College, Cambridge.

At the time of his death, Anthony Masters had completed the typescript of a book on the theatre of the Restoration, commissioned by a publisher who closed down before seeing it into print. After his death, this passed from one firm to another, apparently doomed to gather dust in cupboards — but saved from this fate by the indomitable perseverance of Masters's parents, who were responsible for locating the typescript, repaying the advance, and finding someone of suitable calibre to put the work into final shape, and to match it to the illustrations — most of which had already been selected by the author.

The book is a witty and skilful analysis of the Restoration theatre, which — with the ease that only abundant scholarship can provide — sets out for our enjoyment that small but fascinating world of words and behaviour. The author often lets the characters speak for themselves from the plays, some of which have scarcely seen daylight for centuries. At a time of renewed interest in the period, the appearance of this book is particularly welcome — all the more so since it might so easily have been lost.

Thus it is that, some years after the English theatre was deprived of one of its most sympathetic and knowledgeable connoisseurs, the voice of Anthony Masters again addresses and delights his old friends and, it may confidently be said, wins new ones.

ROGER MORSLEY SMITH

Editor's Introduction

RESTORATION DRAMA invites performance, but resists criticism. Thinking to tempt delicate nineteenth-century appetites to its delights, Charles Lamb suggested that it was 'artificial': and so it was, but not in his sense of being divorced from the real behaviour of real people; for those who inhabited the high society represented in the drama of the age shaped their behaviour by rules of artifice. In our own times, from the 'new critics' of the 1930s to the 'new historicists' of the 1980s, commentators have found it hard to warp the comedy of the times into the weft of their theories. In an extremely influential essay of 1946, L. C. Knights thus took the genre to task for failing his Leavisite test of high seriousness, as if Wycherely should have taken lessons in the portrayal of sexual relationships from D. H. Lawrence. And within the past decade liberal ideologues have found it difficult to accommodate the elitism and sheer brutality of which, undeniably, the Restoration was capable — while feminists have properly deplored the double standards that underlay the outward 'permissiveness' of the period.

An appreciation of Restoration drama — the art form which provided the aptest expression of its age — thus requires a full, almost empathetic understanding of the men and women who shaped it, and of the social milieu by which they in turn were shaped. Since they were of the court and of the town, courtliness and urbanity infused their work — and its 'artificiality' was duly reflected in contemporary modes of performance. In this book, Anthony Masters therefore explores the drama not only through the personalities of playwrights, actors, and managers, but also through the influence exerted by courtiers, courtesans, and even (perhaps especially) the King himself. Radiating a sort of sour and sensual bonhomie from the very epicentre of power and influence, he suggested ideas for plots, culled mistresses from among the actresses his laws had ironically legitimised — and was not above exacting a brutal retribution for a supposed slight from the stage.

Anthony Masters was too happy a stylist and too craftsmanlike a journalist to have left this book 'unfinished' at his death, so its preparation for the press has been a pleasure of the sort rarely afforded an editor all too accustomed to the sloppy punctuation and ploughman's prose of academics. It offers not only a cogent conspectus of its subject, but the privilege of acquaintance with a civilised mind.

SIMON TRUSSLER

1 (opposite). William Morgan's map of London, 1682.

The section shown here, between the City, off to the right, and the Court, off to the left, was fast becoming the most important and influential area of London. As the City merchants gained in confidence to match their wealth, they sought the space and gardens to the west; whilst the Court, realising its need for the wealth of the City, looked to the east. They met in the 'West End' of the City and created in the coffee-houses, taverns, and theatres east of Covent Garden Piazza the fashionable heart of Restoration London.

Although post-dating the Drury Lane theatre, which was opened in 1674, it is believed that the theatre shown on this map between Bridges Street and Drury Lane is the first theatre on that site, which was operating in 1663. Clearly visible is the rotunda, about which Pepys complained on rainy days, and which was such a feature of that theatre. The Duke's Theatre by Dorset Stairs, however, shows the Wren building which opened in 1673. Although Davenant's original theatre in Lincoln's Inn Fields was still standing, it was not in use at this time: it was located in the centre of Portugal Row, just above the 'L' of Lincoln in the title 'Little Lincolns Inne Fields'.

William Morgan was the step-grandson of John Ogilby, who began this major survey of London by proposing his five-volume English atlas in 1669. Ogilby was an interesting and somewhat theatrical figure, and it is entirely in keeping that his entrepreneurial spirit should show us the streets, squares, and houses of the Restoration. He began as a Jacobean court dancer, but ended this career when he broke his leg dancing in a masque for James I in 1621. He taught and eventually opened a school of dancing in Gray's Inn during the early 1630s, and in 1638 he was appointed Master of the King's Revels in Ireland. In this capacity he opened Dublin's first theatre in St Werburgh's Street. He returned to London after the theatre was closed in 1641 — presumably out of work. Probably realising that retraining might be the answer to this politically enforced mid-career caesura, he took up the study of Latin and Greek, and, shortly before the Restoration, he began publishing his own translations of Virgil, Aesop's Fables, and Homer's Iliad.

At the Restoration, Charles appointed him to compose and order the 'Relation of the Entertainments of His Majesty Charles II in His Passage Through the City of London to his Coronation', and he was reappointed Master of the King's Revels in Ireland. He returned to Dublin (this time with Morgan) and established what became Smock Alley Theatre. However, he lost all he possessed at his London base in the Great Fire of 1666, and in the fever of planning and rebuilding he decided to begin what was to prove the most thorough and long-lasting survey map of London. Although he and Morgan achieved considerable encouragement and some financial patronage from the Court of Charles II and the Court of Aldermen of the City of London, and he had working for him a small team of cartographers and draughtsmen, the project was not completed on his death in 1776. Morgan completed the City section (published late in 1676), and issued the more extensive map of London in 1682.

Guildhall Library, London.

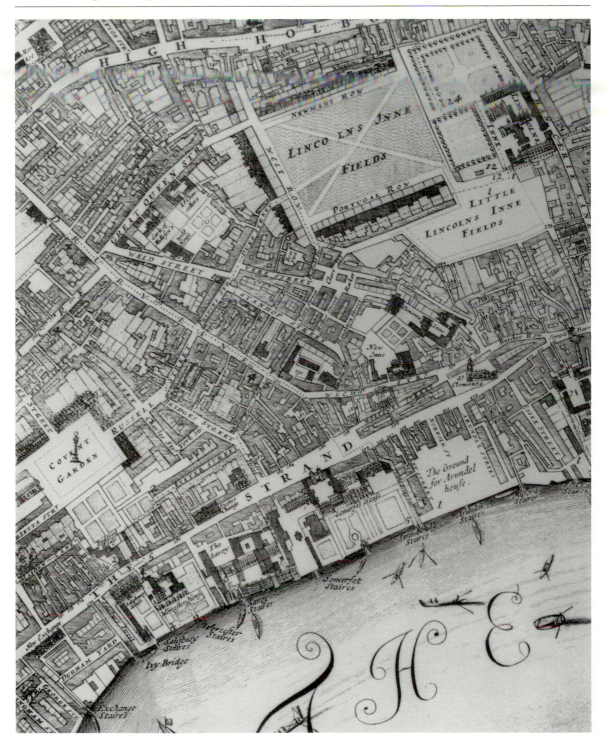

Prologue

RESTORATION THEATRE, as this book seeks to demonstrate, was so intimate an affair that any study of it must incorporate a survey of its personalities. A relatively small group of people, who mostly knew each other, made it what it was. Yet a concern for its lasting value, as well as the need to relieve a long series of biographical sketches, demands consideration of the plays themselves in enough detail to whet the reader's appetite. Hence the dual character of this book.

Of the entire period up to 1710, Anne Barton has remarked that there is much to be said for a study 'which includes everybody, which sets the familiar names in their original context among a host of minor, forgotten dramatists', and considers 'the way in which plays in this tight little artistic world were conditioned by — often specifically written for — particular actors and actresses'. In the space available, I could not include the most minor figures, but I think Mrs Barton's principle has been upheld. The ancillary arts of scenery and music, however, have had to be touched on very briefly.

Society and its drama had changed very significantly within a few years of Charles II's death, and my study goes no further than 1690. Congreve's plays require a book to themselves, to say nothing of those of Vanbrugh and Farquhar. Even Banks and Southerne, while of great interest, belong with the later age: Banks's tragedies on Elizabethan history look forward to Rowe and the sentimental drama of the Augustan period, while Southerne's jaundiced comedies (which, though unsatisfying, have a strongly individual flavour, a sort of Restoration cross between Chekhov and a bitter Noël Coward) left their mark firmly on Congreve's *The Double Dealer* as well as his *The Way of the World*.

A study that tries to be both light and scholarly runs obvious risks, but that combination is what the subject needs. As John Crowne said of one of his plays, 'I do not pretend that [it] wants faults, or that men of sense cannot, with a little pains taking, find matter in it to be displeas'd. . . .' But its intent is wholly serious.

ANTHONY MASTERS

2. Snow Fair on the Thames, 1684, from a contemporary engraving.

*The winter of 1683-84 saw a heavy frost lasting two months, during which the
Thames froze solid and a street of booths was built on it, 'where were sold all sorts
of goods imaginable, namely cloaths, plate, earthenware, meat, drink, brandy,
tobacco, and a hundred sorts of commodities not here inserted: it being the wonder
of this present age and a great consternation to all the spectators'. The various
sports depicted include: (M) 'The Boat drawn with a Hors', (T) 'The Sliding on
Scates', (S) 'The Nine Pinn Playing', and (W) 'The Boyes climbing up the Tree in the
Temple garden to see the Bull Baiting'.*

Hulton Picture Library.

ACT ONE
The King, the Mistresses, and the Courtiers

WHETHER Charles II realised it or not, his return to his kingdom in 1660 perfectly exemplified Aristotle's dramatic idea of total reversal of fortune, accomplished in the most surprising circumstances. The Restoration was the greatest *peripeteia* in the career of Britain's most theatrical monarch. With supreme aptness, it was accompanied by a renaissance of English theatre itself.

As a boy, Charles attended the Court masques so magnificently staged by the brilliant, if stormy, partnership of Ben Jonson and Inigo Jones. His brief stay in Paris during his exile, a moping mature youth at the court of a frigidly dawning Roi Soleil of twelve, must have given him leisure to read, possibly to see, the early productions of France's theatrical golden age. The theatre's rebirth probably took its place in his unfulfilled dreams at that precise moment. Any envy he felt then bore good fruit.

'Merry and scandalous', witty and self-possessed, the restored Charles abounded equally in animal and intellectual energy. Under his patronage, and that of a like-minded aristocracy — frivolous and sterile though many were — the theatre became, as rarely before in modern times, a source of delight uniting practically the whole community, and a genre of artistic expression whose vitality could not be ignored. It painted contemporary society; mirrored its superstars, mocked its failures; and, in the darkening political crises of the reign, provided a barely-disguised battleground for loyalist and republican polemic.

The succession question involving the Catholic Duke of York (eventually to become James II) and Titus Oates's manufactured 'Popish Plot' of 1678 caused a MacCarthyite hysteria such as England has never seen again, which could have ended in bloodiest catastrophe but for Charles's courage, steadfastness, and an ingenuity sometimes bordering on treachery. At this disturbed period, not only did the most distinguished playwright compose the most brilliant political poem in the language (Dryden's *Absalom and Achitophel*), but hardly a play was written without unmistakable indications of the writer's loyalties, whether approached religiously or politically, whether by way of historical reference or brutish satire.

Just as Charles's character expressed that of his age, so it was paralleled by the character of the drama he so actively appreciated. Tolerant, cynical yet kind, he forgave much because, with a dramatist's eye, he understood human nature and enjoyed its rich variety. What he could not tolerate, as both his subjects and servants found from Clarendon downwards, were attempts to regulate himself — from suggestions that Cabinet meetings be held at eight o'clock in the morning to the slightest breath of criticism at the expense of thousands on Nell Gwyn's diamonds and silver bed in years when the impoverished nation had been fighting a war. These were lapses of taste, the only things not to be received with urbanity.

So it is with Restoration comedy. Its timeless grace and style, its superb way with the English language, its debonair wit, render it irresistible to audiences of both sexes and all ages, many of whom ought to find it both offensive and boring, and would be horrified if faced in real life with a burgundy-inflamed Etherege, or a Rochester authentically possessed. Its lusty sensuality, so universally persuasive, is certainly in tune with modern permissive attitudes — which make the strictures editors used to feel obligatory, not to mention their attempts to prove that Mrs Behn's and Dryden's comedies are not really licentious, seem ridiculously archaic. If I did not enjoy these plays myself, I could not have written this book. Yet what should awaken resistance in sensitive readers is a gross masculine chauvinism, a pursuit of pleasure taken to the extreme of ruthless selfishness — however characteristic that, too, is of our own society.

*

At least comedy, in this age, was wholly natural. Its obsessions were those of the audience; tragedy, although lent some interest by a strong preoccupation with romantic love, was peopled only by theatrical stereotypes.

After the high points of Shakespearean, even of minor Jacobean tragic vision, Restoration tragedy marks the beginning of a long, largely unimpressive period in serious English drama, when no attempt was made to connect with the real fears and situations of contemporary society (sexual relations excepted). Tragic poets did not seek to illuminate, or to prove, their audience's less glamorous or reassuring experiences. Safely draped in poetic diction, the representation of passion might still excite, but never disturb. Classical tragedies, misinterpreted so that even an *Oedipus Tyrannus* or a *Hippolytus* would have seemed more august than moving, suggested the ideals of 'theatrical' horror and pity rather than painful and sympathetic involvement. Typically, *King Lear*'s grim denouement was as abhorrent to them as it was to Dr Johnson. To suggest that depiction of real life in all its senselessness might be more powerful and significant than a happy ending would have seemed 'ruder than Gothick'.

In the circumstances, any attempt at arousing emotional involvement was an intolerable lapse of good behaviour. So Dryden's grandeur and fancy, even Lee's frenzy, were acceptable as species of 'wit', understood as flights of intellect; Otway's hysterical despair and (in *The Ambitious Statesman*) Crowne's raw depiction of men's fears, miseries, and treacheries in a royal court seemed almost indecent. Elaborate scenery and music also conspired to turn tragedy into light entertainment. In short, the classic definition of a gentleman as someone who never inflicts pain was one which Restoration tragedians took disastrously to heart.

But the audience — in one respect particularly — were equally to blame. So many Restoration comedies are infuriatingly patchy: brilliant dialogue, and dramatic tension in individual scenes, is not matched by any sustained control over the whole design. (Shadwell and Mrs Behn, though the worst, are not the only offenders). The explanation is not simply that several hands might contribute scenes to the script — which is true — but must be sought in performance conditions. Imagine a houseful of fashionable people, talking and wandering about, flirting and fighting. When conversation flags, or the lady in the box opposite stubbornly refuses to look in our direction, we may attend to the dialogue, and get involved in a connected situation or two. But to hold scenes on a tight rein, to trim dialogue to the bone and calculate the precise sequence of laughs as modern playwrights do, would have been wasted effort.

Writers had no illusions that they could claim the audience's full attention. Since the theatre was a meeting of Court society in plenary session, theatrical performances were tacitly accepted as, so to speak, spanning the footlights. Sometimes, with bitter self-hatred couched in terms resembling highly delicious flattery, dramatists reflected that they were no better than the orange-girls and masked ladies competing with them for the audience's favours:

Old Writers should not for Vain-glory strive;
But, like old Mistresses, think how to thrive.
Be fond of ev'ry thing their Keepers say,
At least till they can live without a Play.

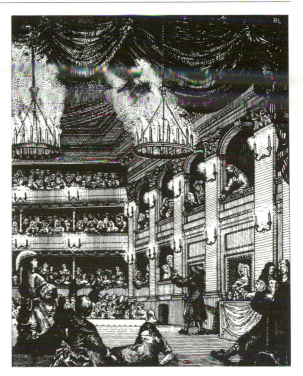

3. The Audience at Drury Lane Theatre, *c.* 1674.

Richard Leacroft skilfully exploited the information from Sir Christopher Wren's longitudinal section of a playhouse (p. 95, below) to create this perspective reconstruction of the interior of the theatre, viewed from the back of the forestage. This gives a clear impression of the way in which the same space and the same light were shared by both audience and actors, and links the Restoration stage closely to the open, platform stages of the Elizabethan and Jacobean theatre.

Richard Leacroft, The Development of the English Playhouse *(London, Eyre Methuen, 1973).*

Like one that knows the Trade, and has been
* hit,*
She dotes and fawns upon her wealthy Cit,
And swears she loves him, merely for his Wit.
Another, more untaught than a Walloon,
Antick and ugly, like an old Baboon,
She swears, is an accomplish'd Beau-garson.
So should wise Poets sooth an aukward Age,
For they are Prostitutes upon the Stage. . . .

*Your Wills alone must their Performance
     measure,
And you may turn 'em every way for Pleasure.*
          Lee, Epilogue to *Theodosius* (1680)

Only in recent times have playwrights found surprising rewards in playing hard to get.

*

But, in fact, it is the intimacy between Restoration authors, performers, and audience which gives the drama its very special brilliance. The Royal Court Theatre of the 1960s — or even the audience of Aristophanes, containing in person all the figures he chose to satirise (who could, like Socrates during the *Clouds*, stand up for identification) — can scarcely compare with the social freedom and unity of Drury Lane and Dorset Garden. Critics, writers, patrons, players did not yet divide themselves into watertight categories; men tried their hand at several roles and were on intimate (often extremely intimate) terms with those playing the others. The audience and cast of a Restoration playwright contained his personal friends and enemies, his mistresses past, present and potential, his cast's lovers or protectors, his rivals as a playwright, and his lords and masters, up to and including the King. He would have to go up to the 1s 6d gallery (the upper circle, in fact) before seeing anyone he did not know, though pursuing the young wives of the middle-aged bourgeois who sat there was almost as satisfying as hunting, and in his plays he often compared the two. This situation could well inspire him to sustained wit, as the presence of one's peers tends to do.

But, again, it would also tend to make his work excessively agreeable.

There were, of course, no daily papers, and no critics in the modern sense. But the jealous rivals and the incompetent scribblers and the pretentious popinjays in the pit formed a solid block of critics which every play had literally to 'get over', far more terrifying than all the inoffensive, mostly serious journalists who occupy end seats at first nights today. The drily devastating asides attributed, in modern times, to Sir Noël Coward and Miss Coral Browne would, in the seventeenth century, have been made at full voice and hysterically applauded. 'Gad', says the unspeakable Sparkish in *The Country Wife*, 'I go to a Play, as to a Country Treat: I carry my own Wine to one, and my own Wit to t'other, or else I'm sure I shou'd not be merry at either.' Wits and critics, said Ravenscroft bitterly, appeared all the year round, even when decent people were purging or on vacation.

This was not all. Sometimes fighting would break out. One man at Dorset Garden was actually killed right in front of the stage; another was stabbed to death by an *ouvreuse*, presumably due to undertipping. One of John Crowne's characters recommended taking out life insurance before a visit to the theatre. But authors generally had to grumble under their breath: the 'stalls public' could not be pressed too far. Or else it was done with such wit and truth that the audience was too delighted to take the hint:

Oh! Sir, you are Governor o' the whole house, no person shall hear any more than your noise pleases; you'll take up six benches in the pit by sprawling, and pay for none of 'em, quarrel with the men, talk scurrilous stuff with the Masques in the hearing of all the Boxes; wrestle with the Orange-maids, throw 'em down, kiss 'em, then offer Ladies o' Quality their leavings. . . .

Crowne, The English Friar, Act IV

Elsewhere, in *The Virtuoso*, Shadwell describes sixteen-year-old sparks 'such as come drunk and screaming into a Play-House, and stand upon the Benches, and toss their full Perriwigs and empty Heads, and with their shrill unbroken Pipes cry, *Damme, this is a damn'd Play: Pr'ythee let's to a Whore, Jack.*' One of them, a little later, murdered the finest actor of his generation.

A very popular innovation was the appearance of women on stage for the first time. 'We may imagine too, that these Actresses were not ill chosen', Cibber observes, 'when it is well known, that more than one of them had Charms sufficient at their leisure Hours to calm and mollify the Cares of Empire.' One only has to think of Nell Gwyn, playing the speech about the King's love in Orrery's *The Black Prince* for all it was worth, or Elizabeth Barry, striding out of rehearsals across the Piazza to meet a more distinguished Earl than yesterday's.

BELLINDA. *But my Glass and I could never yet agree what Face I should make, when they come blurt out with a nasty thing in a Play: For all the Men presently look upon the Women, that's certain; so laugh we must not, tho' our Stays burst for 't, because that's telling Truth, and owning we understand the Jest: And to look serious is so dull, when the whole House is a laughing.*

LADY BRUTE. *Besides, that looking serious does really betray our Knowledge in the matter, as much as laughing with the Company wou'd do. For if we did not understand the thing, we shou'd naturally do like other People.*

BELLINDA. *For my part I always take that Occasion to blow my Nose.*

LADY BRUTE. *You must blow your Nose half off then at some Plays.*

Vanbrugh, The Provok'd Wife, III, iii

But this is only an index of how closely dialogue in drama mirrored the real thing. And here, of course, is the other great charm of Restoration comedy: these people come back from their graves and speak to us. We become part of their social round: bottles of wine at the Cock or the Dog and Partridge, dinner at the French House or Locket's, a stroll in the Mall, a date in the Piazza, an evening in the Spring Garden. It is this society (if I may venture the pun) of which Restoration comedy forms the minutes. What is necessary, therefore, is to meet the most important members one by one; like any series of introductions, it will start by seeming exhausting and mystifying and end, once their contributions and interrelationships are sketched in, with a coherent picture of what Restoration drama was and why.

*

For Charles II, the plays as well as the actresses 'had Charms sufficient . . . to mollify the Cares of Empire'. As John Dennis, playwright and critic, remarked: 'That Monarch lov'd a good Comedy above all Things (excepting one Thing).'

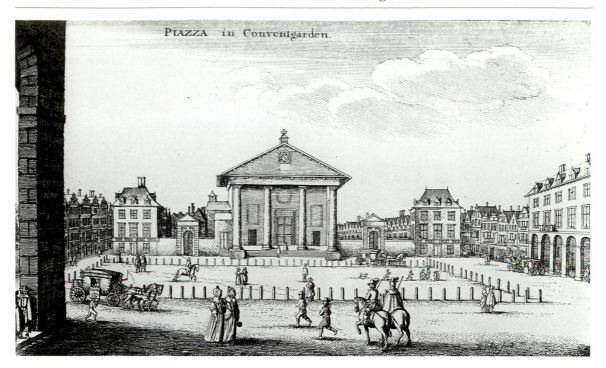

4. Covent Garden Piazza: engraving by Wenceslaus Hollar, probably from the 1640s.

St Paul's Church, finished by Inigo Jones in 1633, dominates the square, as it did before the construction of the former market buildings in the nineteenth century. Contemporary Londoners are depicted strolling or loitering. One wonders how long it will take the cavaliers on the extreme left to accost the ladies who are moving unhurriedly away from them.

Hulton Picture Library.

Like Sedley and Rochester, he supervised every stage of gestation, from suggesting the original idea to polishing and improving dialogue; in the last weeks of his life, he was having regular sessions with Crowne on the script of what became that author's most successful comedy, *Sir Courtly Nice*.

So, too, his mistresses, especially the first and the longest lasting — Barbara Castlemaine, Duchess of Cleveland, who, married in 1659 to a young gentleman of abundant means, is said to have spent the Restoration night of 1660 with the King.

But though she was a quick worker, she built to last. In the networks of patronage and liaison, hers was a unique place. Dryden and Wycherley both began their careers under her wing. Pepys worshipped not only her physical allure, but her position as First Lady. He even dreamt about her. Many of her lovers were connected with the theatre, from a currently lionized rope-dancer or the leading man at Drury Lane to Buckingham and Wycherley — the last an affair which began spectacularly when she called him a son of a whore in Hyde Park. Her com-

5. New Spring Gardens: Victorian print, after an original drawing.

New Spring Gardens, the forerunner of eighteenth-century Vauxhall, were opened soon after the Restoration. Pepys loved to walk there; the heroine of Wycherley's The Gentleman Dancing-Master *deplores not being let out to 'eat a Syllabub' with 'a cousin' there; references to it abound throughout Restoration comedy as an exciting place to spend an evening with friends and perchance to meet new ones.*

Hulton Picture Library.

bination of regal condescension and natural whorishness would have made her the perfect subject for dramatic satire, but she was too powerful. Yet, when Katherine Corey, the Quicklyesque character actress at the Lane, was prohibited

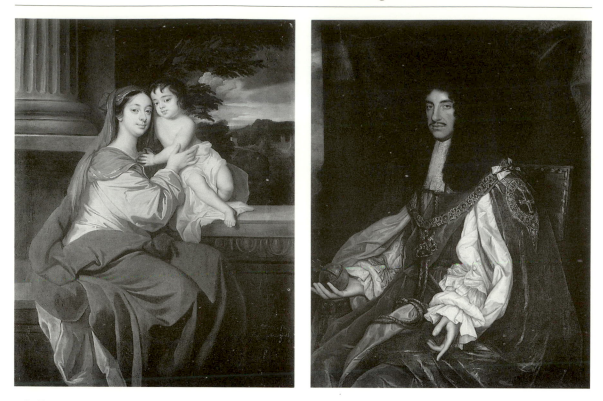

6 (left). Barbara Castlemaine, Duchess of Cleveland: copy after Sir Peter Lely, *c.* 1665-76.

Modestly depicted as the Virgin Mary, Castlemaine here appears with her eldest son by the King. She presented a similar picture to a French convent, much to the nuns' indignation.

7 (right). King Charles II: studio of John Michael Wright.

'That Monarch ', according to John Dennis, 'lov'd a Comedy above all Things (excepting one Thing)'.

National Portrait Gallery, London.

from guying Lady Harvey in one of Newcastle's plays, Castlemaine got the order revoked and instructed her to do it 'worse than ever'.

She lost her position as Sultana of the Court in 1669-70 with the arrival, first of Nell Gwyn, then of the Breton Louise de Quérouaille (later the Duchess of Portsmouth). This completed a petticoat triumvirate destined to survive fifteen years of childbearing, fading looks, and civil upheaval. As we shall see at the end of this book, all three were still together in the last week of Charles's life.

Castlemaine and Nell Gwyn continued to patronise the theatre; even Nelly's accounts for her theatre-parties have survived, though it seems she was never tempted to return to the stage after her early retirement. Charles's eldest child, the Duke of Monmouth, himself an exquisite dancer and his wife a notably good amateur actress, was a particular friend of Dryden. Even the Duke of York joined

8. Jacob Hall: engraving.

This performer, who drew all London to his exhibitions of rope-dancing, was much in demand as 'an Adonis for symmetry, a Hercules for strength'. Castlemaine, an experienced buyer, got her bid in early.

Victoria and Albert Museum, London.

9. The Duchess of Portsmouth in an undress.

Louise de la Quérouaille, Charles II's French mistress, who came over with Louis XIV's embassy in 1670, remained as a favourite for fifteen years, and divided her time at his deathbed between persuading him to embrace Catholicism and trying to get hold of his diamond rings.

Mary Evans Picture Library.

other members of the royal family in lending his most expensive suits to the public theatres, as well as financing productions in the well-used theatre at Court.

So gentlemanly a pastime was the theatre that the King's most distinguished servants did not hesitate to indulge their passion for it. Of these, George Villiers, second Duke of Buckingham, ranked highest in the government, which he effectively led after the fall of Clarendon in 1667. He rose to favour, as you could say his father had done, by tolerating his monarch's vices. He shared the King's tutor in boyhood, matured early (due to his continental upbringing, said Bishop Burnet), and, it was alleged, proceeded to corrupt the King's mind and morals — the former by introducing the subversive and atheistical Hobbes, but the latter presumably by less formal instruction. He actually introduced Charles to Barbara Castlemaine, who was his cousin; and later, one particular lady proving resistant, he and his wife and friends formed a Committee 'for the getting of Mrs Stuart for the King'.

11. George Villiers, second Duke of Buckingham:
Sir Peter Lely, late 1670s.

*According to Dryden, 'A man so various, that he seem'd
to be | Not one, but all Mankinds Epitome', Buckingham
was the King's most theatrical cabinet minister, the
author of the period's most entertaining dramatic satire,
The Rehearsal (1671), and one of the group of Charles's
own contemporaries who came to power in the late 1660s
when the 'old guard' had been deposed.*

National Portrait Gallery, London.

10. The Duchess of Richmond *en travesti*:
Jacob Huysmans, *c*. 1664

*Frances Stewart, for many years, was 'the one who got
away' from the King. Here she appears in male dress,
a playful convention of which art and the theatre made
profitable use (Nell Gwyn was especially popular in
breeches). So resolutely did she resist Charles that his
friends met to discuss ways of solving the problem. At
length she infuriated him by marrying the doltish Duke
of Richmond. Then, in the spring of 1668, the King
apparently paid her a secret visit, clambering over her
garden wall to do so, which Pepys thought 'a horrid
shame'. For three hundred years she appeared as
Britannia on the English penny.*

H. M. the Queen.

Buckingham and Rochester were the
Patroclus and Thersites of Charles II's
court, privileged to rail against 'old
Nestor' — in this case Chancellor Hyde,
Earl of Clarendon, who was irritating the
King with his moral lectures, his excessively serious attitude to government, and
a certain condescension. Buckingham's
talents were singularly varied — in fact,
when Dryden was stung to caricature him
in *Absalom and Achitophel*, it was the very

12. The Life of Buckingham: Augustus Leopold Egg, 1854.

Although wine is flowing freely and there is no great concern shown for the upholstery, this splendidly detailed canvas betrays its mid-Victorian provenance in the decorous theatricality of the composition.

Yale Center for British Art, Paul Mellon Collection.

range of his amateur enthusiasms that he fixed on to such brilliant effect:

In the first Rank of these did Zimri stand:
A man so various, that he seem'd to be
Not one, but all Mankinds Epitome.
Stiff in Opinions, always in the wrong;
Was every thing by starts, and nothing long:
But, in the course of one revolving Moon,
Was Chymist, Fidler, States-Man, and
  Buffoon:
Then all for Women, Painting, Rhiming,
  Drinking;
Besides ten thousand freeks that dy'd in
  thinking.

As 'Buffoon' — which Dryden is probably using in its strict theatrical sense — he achieved one brilliant success, which was actually the cause of Dryden's resentment. His dramatic burlesque, *The Rehearsal* (1671), as well as giving Dryden a nickname, held the stage for a hundred years and more — as late as 1791, a reckless quotation from it by the player-hero producing some splendid complications in *Wild Oats*.

Its technique is familiar, since Sheridan borrowed it for *The Critic* a century later. It purports to portray the rehearsal of a tragedy, proudly watched by its author Bayes (all too obviously Laureate, and hence Dryden) and two more or less sceptical friends. The actor Lacy took pains to imitate Dryden accurately. Certain details tally with what we know of him: his use of the oath 'Gadso', and his practice of clearing out his system with stewed prunes when embarking on a new work. On the first night, Buckingham and Buckhurst even stuck him in a box between them — a typically sadistic touch. But it is not entirely a personal satire: other traits clearly belong to Davenant and the Howards, and the whole character has a coherent insufferability which made Bayes a favourite comic role for star actors throughout the eighteenth century.

The parodied tragic styles, too, cover a wide range, though the Dryden ones are among the best. The blustering hero of *The Conquest of Granada* receives merciless treatment — 'Let petty kings the name of Parties know: Where e'er I come, I slay both friend and foe' — and Dryden's famous simile of two decorously frustrated turtle doves is perverted to picture a couple of pigs noisily copulating in the mud. Moreover, the outlandish South American and North African settings of heroic tragedy

are relentlessly debunked by Buckingham's 'two kings of Brentford' and a fifth act full of romantic West London locations:

GENERAL. *Arm, arm, Gonsalvo, arm; what ho?*
The lye no flesh can brook I trow.
LIEUT. GENERAL. *Advance from* Acton *with the Musquetiers.*
GENERAL. *Draw down the* Chelsey *Curiasiers.*
LIEUT. GENERAL. *The Band you boast of,* Chelsey *Curiasiers,*
Shall, in my Putney *Pikes, now meet their Peers.*
GENERAL. Chiswickians, *aged and renown'd in fight,*
Join with the Hammersmith *Brigade.*
LIEUT. GENERAL. *You'll find my* Mortlake *Boys will do them right,*
Unless by Fulham *numbers over-laid.*
GENERAL. *Let the left-wing of* Twick'nam *Foot advance. . . .*

A subsequent eclipse is staged, much to Bayes's self-satisfaction, by having the Sun, the Moon, and the Earth enter to popular tunes, and do a little dance in which they suitably pass and repass each other.

One is only surprised that the noble Duke didn't take the opportunity of mocking the adulatory dedications as well. Not only was his role as buffoon sustained, but he managed a truly dramatic death. Originally the central 'B' of the *Cabal*, he survived Charles II by a couple of years and then, by a curious accident, expired suddenly in a squalid Yorkshire hovel. The contrast between this and his glittering life inspired the Victorian artist Augustus Egg to a remarkable pair of paintings whose moral intent is only too discernible.

13. The Death of Buckingham: Augustus Leopold Egg, 1854.

The companion picture to that on page 27, heavily reminiscent of the 'Death of Chatterton', lets the spectator ponder the moral as the eye dwells on the almost ghoulishly depicted textures of poverty and degradation.

Yale Center for British Art, Paul Mellon Collection.

But perhaps King Charles's most famous noble courtier was John Wilmot, Earl of Rochester. In every way Rochester is the quintessence of the Restoration: his exuberant talent and personality, his considerable literary gifts, his addiction to sensual pleasures, and, *au fond*, his bitter cynicism and fatalism. The cynicism, expressed with a ruthless wit, got him banished from the Court more than once, but it was too close to the King's own sentiments to cause a permanent breach. His combination of debauchery and an elegant command of language makes him seem the model of a Restoration comedy hero, and, of course, in the *The Man of*

Mode, by his friend Etherege, he actually appeared as one.

He involved himself in the theatre in almost every way short of sustained writing. His tragic scenes are brief and unexciting, his extant attempt at prose comedy stops short at an aimless sub-Etheregean opening speech, and *Sodom*, a vastly entertaining satire of unparalleled obscenity, is rather surprisingly thought not to be his work. But he knew and advised almost every important playwright for a brief period, as well as coaching one major actress to success. 'The best Comic Writers of our Age', wrote Dryden, 'will join with me to acknowledge, that they have copy'd the Gallantries of Courts, the Delicacy of Expression, and the Decencies of Behaviour, from Your Lordship.'

The 'Decencies' Dryden refers to presumably excluded Rochester's frolics of vandalism, wholesale seduction, and murder. More than any of his noble colleagues, Rochester did have a superb command of language that a professional writer would have flogged for all it was worth, and that some professional writers (including Dryden) certainly used. It is no coincidence that one of Dryden's best comedies acknowledges Rochester's active assistance. Yet, at the same time, it is historical fact that practically every playwright found himself taken up for a short time by Rochester and then dropped.

Traditionally, he has been accused of spite, envy, and caprice. But, given a man who could write as perfectly as Rochester is capable of doing in some poems, is it not natural that he should despise the feeble efforts of one writer after another, presuming to make money from their talents, and fawning on patrons for the few extra guineas? His attitude perhaps included envy for those who did actually write so much, as maybe he was too indolent to do. Yet, at its best, his help was both affectionate and materially valuable.

There is scant space here to discuss the disputed evidence for Rochester's behaviour to the poets he patronised. A letter allegedly written by St Evremond, the witty old French *émigré* who certainly knew him and Buckingham, and has even been assigned a share in *The Sullen Lovers,* accuses him of tiring of each protégé in turn; but the hard evidence for it is really a quagmire of disputed identification and authorship within the corpus of Rochester's poems and those of other people. What does seem clearly to have been Rochester's most dominant character trait was his indiscriminate use of his sharp critical faculties. He spared nobody: not Charles II (hence trouble), nor the poet he befriended yesterday. John Crowne dedicated his *Charles VIII* to him in 1672, Rochester satirised him in *Timon* in 1674, and then (very controversially) put him forward for the composition of the Court masque *Calisto* in 1675.

So with Otway, who, it is often said, found himself abandoned by Rochester. Allegedly, the Earl satirised him in a scurrilous poem, *The Session of the Poets*. Easier to prove is that Otway actually satirised Rochester. His description of

---

14. John Wilmot, second Earl of Rochester: after Jacob Huysmans.

'One of the finest men England ever bred, a great and admired Wit but hellishly debauch'd, but made a most extraordinary penitential exit mundo.'

National Portrait Gallery, London.

'that blundering Sot who late a *Session of the Poets* wrote' probably indicates that he thought Settle its author (whoever the author actually was). But what about

Lord Lampoon *and* Monsieur Song,
Who sought her love, and promis'd for 't
To make her famous at the Court. . . .

Who is 'she'? One possibility we shall deal with presently. Or could it even be

He who stunk of that rank Verse
In which he wrote his Sodom *Farce;*
A Wretch whom old diseases did so bite,
That he writ Bawdry sure in spight,
To ruin and disgrace it quite. . . .

This is not a bad description of Rochester's mentality at the end of his life, when melancholia and disgust, not to mention an aching search for religious belief, had taken him over.

The most obvious solution is, like all obvious solutions, partly to be distrusted and probably partly true. It is almost certain that Rochester and Otway were in love with the same woman, the actress Elizabeth Barry. Rochester met her when she was still a girl. When her stage career seemed about to founder almost before it had begun, he taught her to move and speak with that grace which the next two generations were to find incomparable. At first their personal relations were idyllic; then, if we can believe the love-letters, Rochester was disgusted by her coldness and infidelities, and soon terminated the affair. 'Should you lay with her all Night', grumbled the impecunious journalist Tom Brown, 'She would not know you next Morning, unless you had another five Pound at her Service. . . .'

Otway, equally poor, never stood a chance with her; Rochester initially liked Otway and encouraged his early plays, and can hardly have been jealous; but he may well have been irritated to see a woman of such calibre pursued without the requisite poise. Otway's love-letters, with their naked display of emotion, would have aroused as much disgust in Rochester as in Mrs Barry:

Generally with Wine *or* Conversation *I diverted or appeas'd the* Daemon *that possess'd me; but when at night returning to my* unhappy self . . . *every* treacherous Thought *rose up, and took your part, nor left me till they had thrown me on my Bed, and* open'd *those Sluces of* Tears *that were to run till* Morning.

Compare this with a letter of Rochester's, displaying all his style and charm in exquisite cameo:

Madam,
There is now no minute *of my Life that does not afford me some new* Argument *how much I love you; the little* Joy *I take in every thing wherein you are not concern'd, the pleasing* Perplexity *of endless* Thought *which I fall into, where-ever you are brought to my* remembrance; *and lastly, the continual* Disquiet *I am in, during your* Absence, *convince me sufficiently, that I do you* Justice *in loving you so as* Woman *was never* lov'd *before.*

The strongest emotion cannot permit such graces; yet the noble Earl could feel only contempt for those who did not even try to play the game.

The style is certainly irresistible. Yet never for an instant should we underestimate the sheer ruthlessness, the contempt for human suffering, of Rochester and his age. In the words of a hostile but acute witness (Clarendon), 'The Tenderness of the Bowels, which is the Quintessence of Justice and Compassion, the very Mention of good nature, was laughed at and looked upon as the Mark and Character of a Fool; and a Roughness of Manners, or Hardheartedness and Cruelty was affected.' We can see this in the attitude to cuckolds in Restoration comedy — Pinchwife in *The Courtly Wife*, for example. One of the cuckolds Rochester made in real life hanged himself in despair. Nor were the women involved generally shown much 'Compassion'; the misery of the hypersensitive Belinda in *The Man of Mode* is vivid enough to be taken from life.

In short, we may feel that, in the person of the relentlessly selfish Elizabeth Barry, Rochester met his just match. Yet he never forgot that this 'Hardheartedness and Cruelty' was at the least a pose, at most only a part of his nature. And, at the end, moral seriousness, even religious faith, tipped the scale. As Lady Burghclere memorably expressed it, ' "The madcap poet", with the face of a St Sebastian and the vocabulary of a fish-fag, died like a saint in the arms of a Broad Church Bishop.' When we consider the deaths of the age's victims — Otway in poverty, Lee in an asylum — we should not forget Rochester, who, in a poem written with his wife in mind, so eloquently depicted a spirit fighting against the debauchery and cruelty it expected of itself:

Dear, *from thine Arms then let me fly,*
That my Fantastick Mind may prove
The Torments it deserves to try,
That tears my fixt Heart from my love.

When wearied with a world of Woe
To thy safe Bosom I retire,
Where Love, and Peace, and Truth does flow,
May I contented there expire.

Lest once more wandering from that Heav'n,
I fall on some base Heart unblest;
Faithless to thee, False, unforgiv'n,
And lose my everlasting Rest.

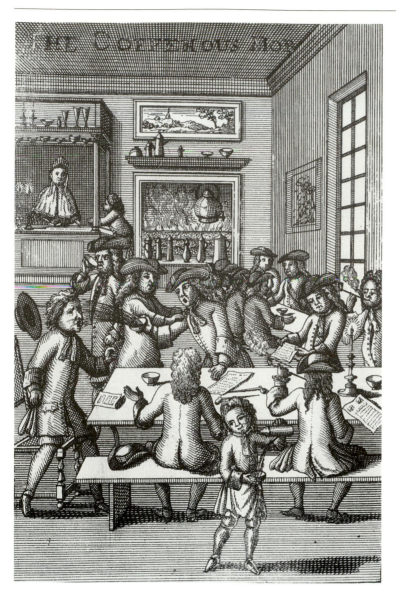

15. A coffee house: from an early eighteenth-century satirical print.

Best remembered nowadays for their civilized literary and political associations in Queen Anne's reign, under Charles II the coffee houses played a more sinister role as hotbeds of 'exclusionist' Whiggery. In 1675 the King actually attempted to suppress them: 'For that in such Houses . . . divers False, Malitious and Scandalous Reports are devised and spread abroad, to the Defamation of His Majesties Government, and to the Disturbance of the Peace and Quiet of the Realm; His Majesty hath thought it fit and necessary, That the said Coffee-Houses be (for the future) Put down and Suppressed [and not] to Utter or sell by retail . . . any Coffee, Chocolet, Sherbett or Tea, as they will answer the contrary at their utmost perils.'

Hulton Picture Library.

ACT TWO
The Gentlemen Playwrights

SO TO our first major playwright, 'gentle' George Etherege. If we ask what Rochester would have written, had he ever completed plays to his liking, Etherege's work (and Wycherley's, which we shall meet presently) supply the answer. They show all Rochester's command of the language, they benefit from the same familiarity with the fashionable behaviour which comedy portrayed, and indeed serve as a likely source for its details.

And so, thanks to *The Country Wife* and *The Man of Mode*, we know fashionable Covent Garden in the 1660s and 1670s as well as we do today's, with its almost comparable modishness. When Dryden holds court on the balcony at Will's Coffee House, between Drury Lane Theatre and what is now the Royal Opera House, and only yards from either; when Greenhill, the greatest portrait painter of the day, whose study of Henry Harris as Wolsey appears on page 90, and who was potentially as much greater than Lely as Goya was greater than Reynolds, died in the gutter in Long Acre before he was thirty, as the playwright Lee was later to do; we feel we are encountering a part of London as familiar as our own.

But Etherege's significance is greater than this. In one supreme masterpiece, he

16. Drury Lane: the corner of Wych Street, and a view down towards the Strand.

This photograph was taken in 1876 from a point where the Aldwych Theatre now stands. The tower of St Mary-le-Strand, not built until 1714, is clearly visible. Before the construction of Kingsway, Aldwych, and Bush House, the quarter still retained its distinct character, with many seventeenth-century buildings remaining which Nell Gwyn must have passed daily. Her own house survived until 1891.

Victoria and Albert Museum, London.

depicted that society with a brilliance even Rochester could scarcely have surpassed. In fact, Rochester and his friends actually appear in *The Man of Mode*, chatting, 'soliciting their Affairs', and generally *chez soi*. Critics objected that Etherege's plays were 'but Translation/Of *Dog and Partridge* Conversation'. So is *The Importance of Being Earnest* a transcription of Café Royal causerie; so is the dialogue of *The Caretaker* seemingly taken down live in Goldhawk Road; the touches by which everyday talk becomes art are no less genuine for being virtually invisible.

Born a vintner's son and apprentice attorney, Etherege rose, through his noble acquaintances and the royal favour with which they brought him into contact, to a knighthood and a distinguished diplomatic career in Regensburg (Ratisbon), writing witty letters, roasting an ox to celebrate William III's accession, and scandalising the local inhabitants by leading the same social life with ladies that he had in Covent Garden thirty years before. It is sad that he left off playwriting, as did Wilde and Congreve, when he had just reached a perfection of ease, economy, and grace that rivals both.

The Comical Revenge, or Love in a Tub (1664) showed his promise, and enabled him to display his personal qualities in society — which constituted a quicker passport to distinction. (Its titles refer to the humiliation inflicted on the French valet Dufoy by infuriated English maids.) Despite some entertaining characters, it is hampered by a schizophrenic plot, of which the other half is not heroic tragedy, but rather stodgy heroic romance.

In his next play, *She Wou'd if She Cou'd* (1668), Etherege created a glorious central character, a middle-aged nympho dame with the explicit name of Lady Cockwood — 'wood' in Restoration type-names being used to mean 'would like' or 'would like to', as in Harwood, Witwood, Woodall. And there are two *jeunes premières* as lively as any in Shadwell or Sir Robert Howard — but one does feel like agreeing, for once, with Pepys who, soured by having a bad seat, found, despite 'something very roguish and witty . . . the design of the play, and end, mighty insipid'. This even though the actors' performance and command of their lines was disastrous, as the author, sitting down front with Buckhurst, Sedley, and Buckingham, openly claimed.

Nothing in these plays prepares us for *The Man of Mode* (1676). In the intervening years, Etherege must have perfected himself still further as courtier and civilised man; yet a positive miracle has transformed his prose. Consider the lovers Dorimant and Belinda, parting at dawn in Act IV, Scene ii:

DORIMANT. *Why will you be gone so soon?*
BELINDA. *Why did you stay out so late?*
DORIMANT. *Call a Chair*, Handy . . . *What makes you tremble so?*
BELINDA. *I have a thousand Fears about me: Have I not been seen, think you?*
DORIMANT. *By no Body but my self and trusty* Handy . . . *What does that Sigh mean?*
BELINDA. *Can you be so unkind as to ask me? well* — (Sighs.) *Were it to do again* —
DORIMANT. *We should do it, should we not?*
BELINDA. *I think we should; the wickeder Man you, to make me love so well* — *Will you be discreet now?*
DORIMANT. *I will* . . .
BELINDA. *You cannot.*
DORIMANT. *Never doubt it.*

BELINDA. *I will not expect it.*
DORIMANT. *You do me wrong.*
BELINDA *You have no more Power to keep the Secret, than I had not to trust you with it.*

The 'portraits from life' in *The Man of Mode* make it the quintessence of Restoration comedy. Dorimant, whose amours provide a rather pliable backbone for the plot, makes his first entrance with a quote from Waller that instantly identifies him with Rochester, who loved the poet. 'It was unanimously agreed', says John Dennis, 'that he had in him several of the qualities of Wilmot, Earl of Rochester, as, his wit, his spirit, his amorous temper, the charms that he had for the fair sex, his falsehood, and his inconstancy; the agreeable manner of his chiding his servants, which the late Bishop of Salisbury takes notice of in his life' — quoting Waller. But, despite the 'unanimity' Dennis alleges, so typical was Dorimant of the Restoration bravo that various identifications were suggested, Buckhurst among them.

Medley, the hero's sidekick who gets few of the ladies but most of the best lines, is clearly Sir Charles Sedley, poet, playwright, and fellow-debauchee of Etherege and Buckhurst, notable in the 'Oxford Kate's' episode of 1663. This, one of the reign's great exhibitions, involved the three drunken gentlemen enjoying a dinner served by six topless waitresses, cavorting naked on the balcony of a Covent Garden whorehouse, preaching blasphemous sermons and 'blessing' an increasingly large crowd with the contents of claret bottles, purposely refilled with what was certainly not holy water.

Sir Fopling Flutter, one of the first and greatest of Restoration fops, represents the famous Beau Hewitt (who, in addition to his extravagances of dress, beat up Ravenscroft one night at the Theatre Royal and caused a fracas in which no less a person than Buckhurst was wounded). The wanly amorous Young Bellair is said to be a portrait, presumably toned down, of Etherege himself. Even the London shoemaker of Act I, a true natural with his irreverent wit and foul abuse of the French, was drawn from life and found the publicity highly profitable. But, strangely enough, no real-life identification has been suggested for Harriet, the witty and astute heroine whose sanity and self-possession bring the hero to heel, and, foreshadowing the Cynthia and Angelica of the 1690s, gives the play much of its Congrevean atmosphere.

Sir Fopling displays, of course, that obsession with French modes without which no fop would earn ridicule, and in his first scene delightedly undergoes a catechism of questions about his wig, gloves, hat, and so on — thus providing modern scholars with the Restoration equivalents for Gucci, Ted Lapidus, and Smile. Typically, in Act IV, Scene i, his affectation extends to being coy about his social accomplishments:

HARRIETT. *I had rather see you dance yourself, Sir* Fopling.
SIR FOPLING. *And I had rather do it — all the Company knows it —but Madam —*
MEDLEY. *Come, come, no Excuses, Sir Fopling.*
SIR FOPLING. *By Heav'ns*, Medley . . .
MEDLEY. *Like a Woman, I find you must be struggl'd with, before one brings you to what you desire.*

The climax of grotesquerie is reached in

17. Thomas D'Urfey: John van der Gucht.

*D'Urfey was Buckhurst's librarian at Knole, but always
something of a poor relation. He wrote some enjoyable
comedies, of which* Madame Fickle; or, The Witty
False One *(1676) and* Love for Money; or, The
Boarding School *(1691) are probably the best. They
show great flair for character, and many of his later
works are a Shadwellian parade of delicious grotesques —
often not quite making a play, but fun to read.*

Knole.

find this same love-hate attitude to
libertinism when we come to Wycherley.)
Is it really, as the brilliant American
scholar Harriett Hawkins has suggested, a
subtle seventeenth-century essay on the
importance of maintaining one's cool in a
fashionable affair?

In performance, holding the audience's
attention through Dorimant's slight and
labyrinthine adventures poses a severe
problem; like so many Restoration plays, it
implicitly asks to be watched scene by
scene without worrying unduly about the
larger structure. But the effortless grace of
its dialogue remained unequalled till *Love
for Love*; and its austere conclusion, when
Harriet draws a proposal of marriage from
the rakish hero and then, like the heroines
of *Love's Labour's Lost*, demands a period
of penance to make him worthy of her,
makes a serious comment on Restoration
mores that is less ambitious, and yet much
more successful, than Wycherley's in his
own last play. Perhaps, after it, another
Etherege play was neither necessary nor
possible.

*

his flirtation with the revealingly named
Mrs Loveit, a magnificent role for Mrs
Barry at her bitchiest — coquettish, foul-
tempered, and desperately lonely, but
constantly losing our sympathy and
raising our laughter with her tempests of
furious tears.

Yet, for all its colour and wit, *The Man of
Mode* is a strangely elusive play. What *are*
its feelings towards Dorimant and his
hedonistic attitude to women? (We shall

Charles Sackville, Lord Buckhurst and
later sixth Earl of Dorset, derives his
literary reputation from poetry alone,
but he perfectly exemplifies the period's
sympathetic and deeply involved patrons
of the theatre. Seventeen years old at
the Restoration, he became the centre of
the Etherege-Sedley group, as noted for
rowdy behaviour as for poetic refinement.
He was a favoured international diplomat;
he embellished Knole, one of his country
houses, with magnificent furniture and a
fine collection of portraits of the literary

18. Beau Wilson *en pleine tenue*.

One of the later 'Restoration' fops, c. 1690, casually displaying his latest carefully studied clothes.

Mary Evans Picture Library.

gentlemen whom he loved to invite there, and overwhelm with his generosity.

On one occasion the poor scribblers found fifty-pound notes silently pushed under their plates at dinner; and it is said that Dryden, invited to judge an epigram contest, had no trouble in deciding for his lordship's own entry, which read: 'I promise to pay John Dryden, Esq., or order, on demand, the sum of five hundred pounds. Dorset.' 'I must confess', said Dryden, 'that I am equally charmed with the style and the subject.'

With an incestuousness typical of this period, Buckhurst's most celebrated affair was with Nell Gwyn. In 1667 (she was only sixteen at the time, he still in his twenties), he drew her away from Drury Lane and Charles Hart, her current lover, and set her up in an establishment at Epsom with a room for Sedley. 'They keep a merry house', noted Pepys disapprovingly. In fact, it only lasted a few weeks; Nell was soon back at Drury Lane acting a Dryden tragic lead way beyond her talents. But Hart (or so Pepys was told by Orange Moll at the theatre, clearly as good a gossip as the orange-woman in *The Man of Mode*), refused to resume their relationship, leaving the field open for royal artillery. Buckhurst, to whom the King was invariably generous, lost no sleep over the departure of his playmate, and he and Sedley were soon 'running up and down with their arses bare through the streets, and at last fighting', much as before.

Waller (among others) collaborated with him and Sedley on his sole dramatic work, a translation of Corneille's *Mort de Pompée*, produced at St James's Palace and subsequently at the Duke's theatre. With his friends, the King included, he was a first-night connoisseur who would often manage (as with *The Plain Dealer*) to influence the audience towards a reasonable reaction — of which, at premieres, they are so seldom naturally capable. His importance was out of all relation to his output: Rochester called him 'the best good *Man*, with the worst natur'd *Muse*'. In another place he remarked, very revealingly, 'I do not know how it is, My Lord Dorset might do anything, he is never to blame.' (This presumably included spending his time as Lord Chamberlain drinking ale all day with Shadwell at Dorset Garden, as a letter from Nelly records.) He died in 1706, having lived long enough to be the dedicatee of Congreve's *Love for Love* and help to found the Kit-Cat Club. Alexander Pope wrote his epitaph:

The scourge of pride, though sanctified or great,
Of fops in learning, and of knaves in state . . .
Blest courtier! who could King and country please,
Yet sacred kept his friendship and his ease. . . .

The last and greatest member of this aristocratic group of friends was William Wycherley — as personable and witty a gentleman as any of his heroes. Like Etherege, he owed his social position to a well-written but slight first play. The success of *Love in a Wood* about 1671 led to an affair with Castlemaine, following a bravura pick-up as their coaches passed in Hyde Park. His period as her escort and protégé did not preclude friendship with the King, who had deserted her for Nell

19 (opposite page). William Wycherley: after Sir Peter Lely.

National Portrait Gallery, London.

Gwyn and Moll Davis some time previously. Indeed, Charles actually went to his lodgings when he was ill, and gave him five hundred pounds to convalesce in the south of France. Very likely his plays also benefited from Charles's suggestions to an extent which we cannot now determine.

His modern reputation rests on *The Country Wife* (1675) — a play that triumphantly combines some scintillating dialogue, clever farcical plotting, and bitterly Jonsonian satire. Even when the eighteenth century found the gleeful seduction of an innocent bride altogether too gamey, Garrick's charming little bowdlerisation remained popular, and it is still the most widely enjoyed of Restoration comedies. What makes it a great play, as well as an entertaining one, is its strange ambiguity. At one level, it features some of the best 'Dog and Partridge conversation':

HARCOURT. *No, Mistresses are like Books; if you pore upon them too much, they doze you, and make you unfit for Company; but if us'd discreetly, you are the fitter for conversation by 'em.*
DORILANT. *A Mistress shou'd be like a little Contry retreat near the Town, not to dwell in constantly, but only for a night and away; to taste the Town the better when a Man returns.*
HORNER. *I tell you, 'tis as hard to be a good Fellow, a good Friend, and a Lover of Women, as 'tis to be a good Fellow, a good Friend, and a Lover of Money: You cannot follow both, then choose your side; Wine gives you liberty, Love takes it away.*
DORILANT. *Gad, he's in the right on 't.*
HORNER. *Wine gives you joy, Love grief and tortures, besides the Chirurgeon's: Wine*

makes us witty, Love only Sots: Wine makes us sleep, Love breaks it. . . . For my part I will have only those glorious, manly pleasures of being very drunk, and very slovenly.

Superficially viewed, the play's action is similar — delightfully hedonistic. Its 'hero' Horner's scheme of getting himself reputed a eunuch to facilitate access to married women may be borrowed from Roman comedy, but the richness of character and situation, the delight in sex and in language, gives the play a vigour which makes *The Man of Mode* seem very restrained, and renders this a uniquely graphic picture of Restoration behaviour. Indeed, Horner, Mrs Pinchwife and several other characters were, it seems, closely based on friends of Wycherley's in Wiltshire.

At the same time, there is an underlying detachment, even disgust, which gives the most sparkling prose an agreeable acid flavour.

SIR JASPER. *Come, come, Man; what, avoid the sweet society of Woman-kind? that sweet, soft, gentle, tame, noble Creature Woman, made for Man's companion —*
HORNER. *So is that soft, gentle, tame, and more noble Creature a Spaniel, and has all their tricks; can fawn, lye down, suffer beating, and fawn the more; barks at your Friends, when they come to see you; makes your bed hard, gives you Fleas, and the mange sometimes: and all the difference is, the Spaniel's the more faithful Animal, and fawns but upon one Master.*

Horner's plan succeeds brilliantly; as he remarks, 'your Women of Honour, as you call 'em, are only chary of their reputations, not their Persons, and 'tis scandal they wou'd avoid, not Men.' By Act IV the women of honour are offering themselves in a profusion he finds hard to conceal, and harder to satisfy. In the play's most famous scene, his pretence that they have come to see his china collection leads to the most dazzlingly sustained passage of *double entendre* in English comedy.

One cannot help enjoying this enormously: but Wycherley's own feelings are divided. As in a Ben Jonson play like *Volpone*, piling on the comic action in this bitterly satiric vein is simultaneously exciting and chilling. There are no delicate Dorimant-Belinda partings here. Michael Redgrave, who acted in the 1936 Old Vic production, has spoken of the 'nastiness' of the play; and his frustration when Tyrone Guthrie insisted on Horner being played as a 'fresh young man' to 'get it past Lilian Baylis and the board of governors' does him great credit, especially considering the date.

It is not simply Horner's character that creates this impression, but the innocence of the country wife he corrupts — let alone the pathetic figure of Pinchwife, who has been a whoremaster in his time, but becomes a homicidally jealous husband who threatens to blind her and carve 'whore' in her face with his penknife. Wycherley's breezy sensuality was genuine, but he knew its effects. Indeed, he suffered them a few years later when he met a Countess leafing through his works in a Tunbridge Wells bookshop, married her, and then found she insisted on the windows at the Cock Tavern being open when he was there, to show there were no women present, or 'she would be immediately in a downright raging condition'.

His last play, *The Plain Dealer* (1676) takes this bitterness to its limits. It is a flawed masterpiece, word-clogged but memorably sombre, that modern directors have been understandably reluctant to stage. The keynote is struck by the misanthropic hero, Manly, in a magnificent opening sentence: 'Tell not me (my good Lord *Plausible*) of your *decorums*, supercilious forms, and slavish Ceremonies; your little Tricks, which you, the Spaniels of the World, do daily over and over, for and to one another; not out of Love or Duty, but your servile Fear.' Lord Plausible replies, with a significant change of rhythm from tramping to tripping, 'Nay, i'faith, i'faith, you are too passionate; and I must humbly beg your Pardon and Leave to tell you, they are the Arts and Rules the Prudent of the World walk by.'

Familiar? Of course. Here, in British periwigs and honest kersey, are Molière's Alceste and Philinte (unacknowledged). Replacing the marquesses and the dangerous poetaster of *Le Misanthrope*, we have Plausible ('a ceremonious, supple, commending Coxcomb'), Major Oldfox ('an old impertinent Fop'), the 'pert railing Coxcomb' Novel, not to mention the Widow Blackacre, a litigious old trout whose endless chatter owes something to Lady Politick Would-Be in *Volpone*. Finally, *la belle Célimène* becomes the vicious and hypocritical Olivia, whose railings against the court and town, closely echoing Manly's when it suits her, mask unparalleled depths of perfidy and affectation.

For Manly, society is a grotesque Paul Jones of insincerity: 'Here you see a Bishop bowing low to a gaudy Atheist; a Judge to a Door-Keeper; a great Lord to a

20. Westminster Hall: an early eighteenth-century engraving.

This print shows the bookstalls, picture stalls, and other shops which formerly turned Westminster Hall from a house of law into a den of thieves, presenting such a strange picture to modern eyes. The third act of The Plain-Dealer, *in which the Widow Blackacre perpetually pursues serjeants, barristers, and the like, while her son Jerry is distracted by the displays of ephemera, brings such a scene to life.*

Mary Evans Picture Library.

Fishmonger, or Scrivener with a Jack-Chain about his Neck; a Lawyer to a Serjeant at Arms; a Velvet Physician to a Thread-bare Chymist; and a supple Gentleman Usher to a surly Beef-Eater; and so tread round in a preposterous Huddle of Ceremony to each other, whilst they can hardly hold their solemn false Countenances.' He totally ignores Fidelia, the one character who really loves him.

Though a pale and unconvincing plagiary of Viola in *Twelfth Night*, Fidelia is important as showing that Wycherley felt it necessary to believe in innocence, or just to introduce an innocent character to prevent the play's blackness from getting out of control. Elsewhere, his comic writing often excels itself, with Molière's blueprint, sometimes Molière's actual lines, subsumed into something wholly Restoration and very British. A favourite Molière joke (in *Dom Juan*, *Le Malade Imaginaire*, and so on), that of referring scathingly to his own plays, suggests Olivia's sanctimonious strictures on the china scene in *The Country Wife*, and Célimène's famous hit at Alceste —

Et ses vrais sentiments sont combattus par lui,
Aussitôt qu'il les voit dans la bouche d'autrui

— receives a further twist: 'Your Opinion is your only mistress, for you renounce that too, when it becomes another Man's.'

The caricatures are drawn with a Jonsonian zest and venom. But here again, it is unmistakably a last play. Though a satisfactory ending is contrived, and though one quite agrees with Freeman (the real equivalent of Philinte) that 'most of our Quarrels to the World, are just such as we have to a handsome Woman; only because we cannot enjoy her as we wou'd do', Manly still concludes:

Yet, for my sake, let no one e'er confide
In Tears or Oaths in Love, or Friend untry'd.

The only development possible was Rochester's deathbed; and, of course, Wycherley's opinion of the world's Bishop Burnets was as cynical as his view of everything else.

*

Roger Boyle, Earl of Orrery and brother of the great scientist Robert Boyle, comes into the category of the Important Historical Figure. 'A Man who never made a bad figure but as an Author' — Horace Walpole's bitchy description deserves to be taken seriously. Yet his influence was significant. The reign's great controversy of taste, over the merits of rhyme and blank verse in tragedy — really a question of French tradition versus English — directly inspired his rhymed plays, which were written at the King's personal suggestion and enjoyed a brief vogue in the 1660s. Once again, Orrery was a man of action, and his plays were pure therapy, undertaken during fits of gout. He was at the time Lord President of Munster, but also a Member of Parliament who could visit London periodically when the King had his work staged.

Orrery had great energy — and presumably some charm, since Charles II didn't sit up gaming with bores. But his works are charmless, entirely humourless, and largely undramatic. They suggest a Corneille devoid of theatrical skill and poetic inspiration, and would seem to be written for the study rather than the stage — if only they were readable. But his influence on Dryden must be reckoned with — first towards imitation, then to reaction. The torch was actually passed to Dryden by a similar figure to Orrery — Sir Robert Howard, a relation of Orrery's by marriage, as was Thomas Killigrew, the manager at Drury Lane.

As Secretary to the Treasury and Auditor of the Receipt, Robert Howard took professional versatility as far as, even in this period, it could go. Simultaneously with demolishing Clarendon in the House of Commons and being largely responsible for his fall in 1667, he was a lessee of the

21 and 22 (this page and opposite). 'Solyman's Tent' and 'Buda Beleagured: the Common'.

Two original set designs by John Webb for a production of Orrery's tragedy Mustapha *at Whitehall Palace in 1665.*

Chatsworth.

Theatre Royal, wrote several plays, had a literary squabble with his brother-in-law Dryden (a claim to attention, if not to uniqueness), and, most interestingly for us now, was caricatured by Shadwell as Sir Positive At-All in *The Sullen Lovers* (1668).

It is the liveliest portrait of him we have. This wonderful character, whose Jonsonian name is worthy of its grand scale, transforms and takes over an indifferent play with a virtuoso display of outrageous vanity, pedantry, and petulance. (In real life, Evelyn found Sir Robert 'not ill-natured, but insufferably boasting'.) Sir Positive's non-stop verbal flow on all subjects may, indeed, remind us of one or two know-alls in the public eye today — as witness the following passage from Act IV. Wearied beyond endurance by his polymathic pretensions, the other characters fire a volley of topics off faster than he can deal with them. Not till they pause for breath has he a chance to make up for lost time:

SIR POSITIVE. *Hold, hold, hold, hold! Navigation, Geography, Astronomy, Palmestry, Physick, Divinity, Surgery, Arithmetick, Logick, Cookery and Magick: I'll speak to every one of these in their Order; if I don't understand 'em every one in Perfection, nay, if I don't Fence, Dance, Ride, Sing, fight a Duel, speak* French, *command an Army, play on the Violin, Bag-pipe, Organ, Harp, Hautboy, Sackbut, and double Curtal, speak* Spanish, Italian, Greek, Hebrew, Dutch, Welsh *and* Irish, *Dance a Jig, throw the Bar, Swear, Drink, Swagger, Whore, Quarrel, Cuff, break Windows, manage Affairs of State, Hunt, Hawk, Shoot, Angle, play at Cat, Stool-ball, Scotch-hop and Trap-ball, Preach, Dispute, make Speeches* — [Coughs] *Pr'ythee get me a Glass of Small-beer,* Roger.

STANFORD. *Hell and furies!*

EMILIA. *Oh, oh . . .* [They run.]

SIR POSITIVE. *Nay, hold, I have not told you half; if I don't do all these, and fifty times more, I am the greatest* Owl, Pimp, Monkey, Jack-a-napes, Baboon, Rascal, Oaf, Ignoramus, Logger-head, Curr-dog, Blockhead, Buffoon, Jack-pudding, Tony, *or what you will; spit upon me, kick me, cuff me, lugg me by the Ears, pull me by the Nose, tread upon me, and despise me more, than the world now values me.*

The picture was horribly accurate; Sir Robert never lived it down. But it should not blind us to his real talents and importance. His best-known work, *The Indian Queen* (1664), was a collaboration with Dryden in which he may have had much the largest share; at all events, it is a beautifully accomplished piece of dramatic and poetic writing, within the canons of the time. *The Duke of Lerma* (1668), his other great tragedy, shows even greater dramatic skill, though there is once again a problem in assigning the credit since it is largely a reworking (at the suggestion of Charles Hart) of a play submitted to the Theatre Royal in manuscript — possibly an old play whose author was not alive to rewrite or claim the praise. But if Howard's remarks on the original plot are fair, some of the best scenes are his. And what is quite clear is that, before Dryden achieved full recognition, Howard was virtually the Drury Lane dramaturg in addition to his activities in public life.

He also had a gift for spirited comedy. *The Committee* (1662) looks back satirically to Cromwellian times — always an easy way to success in the safety of Charles II's London, as was the mockery of grave 'city Fathers' and their Whiggish, anti-Royalist policies, into which it imperceptibly merged. The play is rich in comic characters — the literal-minded Irishman Teg, who, when asked to take the covenant, purloins it from the nearest bookstall; the slow and pompous Obadiah, Clerk to the Committee, who is filled up with sack by Teg, flung incapable into a sedan, and deposited in his respectable Puritan home bawling royalist drinking songs.

Even Howard's minor comedy, *The Country Gentleman* (1669), whose inspirations include the memorably named Mistress Finical Fart, was enlivened with scenes of outrageous satire from Buckingham's hand. Sir William Coventry was the target; as we know from Pepys, who appreciated his conscientiousness, he was a very serious-minded minister whose sole vanity was his contribution to office furniture, a revolving table with a hole in the middle, enabling the Restoration executive to summon books and papers on any subject with a whirl of the mechanism. Buckingham, typically, introduces *two* pompous old men, whirling two work-tables round in frenzied competition. This crude but very funny episode was enough to get *The Country Gentleman* banned, and in fact it was presumed lost until, in 1976, it was discovered, edited, and published by two American scholars, Scouten and Hume.

The Sullen Lovers also makes short work of Edward Howard, Sir Robert's brother and author of a number of indigestible plays produced at the Lane about this time, in the character of Ninny, 'a conceited Poet [using] such affected Words, that 'tis as bad as the Canting of a Gypsie'. But another brother, James, was an exceedingly able comic writer. *The English Mounsieur* (1663) is notable for its title role, who anticipates Wycherley's ludicrously Frenchified Monsieur de Paris by nearly ten years. Less well known is its enchanting scene of rival courtship, in the tradition of Touchstone and William in *As You Like It*, or Molière's Dom Juan, Pierrot, and Charlotte (still to be written), showing Wiltshire clown and London gentleman in competition over a country lass — a classic instance of the great confrontation between Art and Nature, town and country, simplicity and artifice. While Mr Comely's declaration of love to Elsba is Restoration courtesy run mad, the flowers of rhetoric burgeoning into an impenetrable jungle, William's has an irresistible naivety and freshness:

23. Sir William Coventry: John Riley.

His plain speaking in Parliament brought him trouble when he suggested that the King's concern for the theatre might be more a matter of interest in actresses: on his way home he was attacked and had his nose cut to the bone. When satirized by Buckingham in a play, Sir William challenged him to a duel; he was immediately put in the Tower, where Pepys commiserated with him, but succeeded in getting the play banned.

Longleat.

Elsba, I do love Thee, I find by the com-
fashiousness of my heart, I could suck thy Eyes
out of thy head, I could eat thy lips though I
were not an-hungard, I could lick thee all over
as our Cow does her Calf. O Elsba, my heart do
Thunderclap my breast when I think o' thee, a
wou'd methinks sometimes though I never am
anger'd with thee, I could tear the cloaths off
thy back, Smock and all, my heart does leap
and caper when I do see this leg and thy Coats
tuck't up as thou com'st home from Milking
Vathers Kine. . . .

The charming honesty of this passage,
which still enables the London fops to
laugh if they wish, shows Howard's skill
and does much to atone for the easy
mockery of rustic simplicity to which the
rest of Restoration comedy was prone.
Anyhow, he has a laugh in store for the
fops: Elsba chooses the rustic.

Finally, James Howard's great tragi-
comedy, *All Mistaken, or The Mad Couple*
(1667), gave Nell Gwyn, then sixteen and
at the start of her career, a perfect role as the
witty, insouciant Mirida, with an appropriate opposite number Philidor (probably
Charles Hart). Howard might even have
had her in mind when he made Mirida
say, 'I'm now / But five years i' th' Teens,
and I have fool'd / Five several men.'

Mirida is also involved in a double *My
Fat Friend* situation, tormenting a very fat
and a very skinny admirer by insisting
that they respectively lose and gain
weight. There is much lavatory humour,
too: Pinguister's slimming programme
involves drastic laxatives, which neces-
sitate sudden exits from the stage at what
might suitably be called regular intervals.
There is also an absurd non-love-scene
between him and tiny Nell — a sort of
Osmin and Blonda in monochrome. Separ-
ated from him by the width of the Drury
Lane stage, she humiliates him with impossible demands, such as that he roll
across in under two hours, and sings a
plaintive song about his 'Grease' which
unmistakably parodies the air that gave
her great rival, catty little Moll Davis, an
opening to the King's infatuation. (As
yet another illustration of the Restoration
theatre's incestuousness, Pepys says that
Moll was the bastard daughter of yet
another Howard brother.) Needless to say,
the town adored the play.

ACT THREE
The Professionals

WITH John Dryden, we finally cross the line from the patrons to the patronised. Though he did marry a sister of the Howards, and could honestly call himself a personal friend of Sedley, Buckhurst, and Rochester, Dryden remained very much the professional author, often struggling, always at patrons' mercy. (The payment of his salary as Laureate often got years in arrears.) None of his plays have really held the stage, but such is the variety, volume, and interest of his work, both in itself and seen as part of the period, that a summary in small space is extremely difficult.

He was the most important playwright of his times, and knew those times very well. To us, who admire his *Absalom and Achitophel* for its superb craftsmanship, poise, and wit, it may seem a pity that the plays which took up so much energy throughout his life don't display the same genius. If he had been born in another century (the eighteenth or nineteenth, for example), he would probably not have been drawn to the stage. Yet, like so many of the gentlemen playwrights, he had a natural feel for it, both in tragedy and comedy. What never came was a plot, or even a genre of play, which could have exploited his brilliant gift for irony and sarcasm in poetic terms. Verse comedies were always rare: Crowne's *The Married Beau*, which nearly comes off, belongs to 1694, just as Dryden stopped writing. And while his comic dialogue in prose can be superb, it has the unmistakable air of doing well what everybody else did well; and, rightly, we expect more from John Dryden.

Personally and artistically, he was full of contradictions. Elected Poet Laureate on Davenant's death in 1668, his life was largely spent, not on some Parnassian eminence, but amid the guerrilla or jungle warfare into which politics, touchy personalities and the theatre's irrational reversals of fortune too often dragged literary men. Professional quarrels, snubs real or imagined, and rivalries were constant, and Dryden was always deep in whatever there was. The 'Zimri' passage on Buckingham has been quoted already, and his devastating attacks on Shadwell are equally well-known. 'If you are Inquisitive to know why there are such continual Picques amongst the *Poets*,' wrote Ravenscroft in 1673, 'I can give you no other Reason than what one Whore told the other — *Two of a Trade can seldome agree*.'

It actually indicates how deeply writers cared about their art. Dryden was by nature a perfectionist, often forced to compromise yet infuriated at seeing inferior writers succeed, desperately in need of constant praise. (This emotional intensity as an artist was itself a breach of decorum, which did not help him.) Writers as different as the neurotic Lee and the gentlemanly Congreve attest to Dryden's warm friendship and appreciation, but he could also be very jealous and ungenerous — first joining with Crowne against Settle, then, when Crowne had a success, alleging that his own father and Crowne's mother had been 'very well acquainted'. He was vain, to which his noble patrons did not take kindly. He told Swift frankly that 'the World would never have suspected him to be so great a Poet, if he had not assured them so frequently in his Prefaces, that it was impossible they could either doubt or forget it.'

His most controversial act, his conversion to Roman Catholicism after the accession of James II, was understandably criticised then and since (it was suggested that both his pen and his wife were for sale at the right price), but may have genuinely sprung from his complex emotional nature and religious thinking. If so, he suffered for it; for when William of Orange restored protestantism in 1689 Dryden lost the laureateship and had the galling experience of watching Buckhurst (who was still subsidising him) bestow it on the hated and despised, genial, hard-drinking Shadwell.

His career, like many others, began with an indifferent play, championed by a powerful patron (in this case Castlemaine herself) and leading to social and literary opportunities. In the 1660s, when his relationship with the Howards was close,

he produced mainly comedies and tragi-comedies — a genre for which he retained an inexplicable fondness. Of these early works, the most promising is *The Indian Queen* (1664), his collaboration with Sir Robert Howard. But it almost seems as though he could not produce his own strain of tragedy until the failure of Orrery's *Tryphon* (1668) suggested something more sensational, in language, in staging, and in its whole emotional range.

Four subsequent full-length tragedies in rhyming couplets — *Tyrannick Love* (1669), the two parts of *The Conquest of Granada* (1670-71), and *Aureng-Zebe* (1675) — are at the highest point of English heroic tragedy. *All for Love* (1677), which is greater still, takes Shakespeare's *Antony and Cleopatra* as a starting point for an experiment with blank verse, less formalism, and fewer heroic sentiments. It is unfortunate in a way that this is Dryden's best-known tragedy, because it is quite untypical, but the impact of his new dramatic language makes one regret that he did not pursue it further.

Its only successor is *Troilus and Cressida, or Truth Found Too Late* (1679), a revealing mature experiment in trying to 'tidy up' Shakespeare without complete rewriting. As well as cutting all obsolete words, pruning the luxuriance of Shakespeare's poetic fancy, and clarifying the clogged language with which, in this play especially, he labours to express his characters' various political and emotional difficulties, Dryden added a magnificent scene for Betterton and Smith (as Troilus and Hector respectively), which is heavily indebted to Brutus and Cassius's quarrel in *Julius Caesar* but none the worse for that, and provided a virtuous motivation for the

24. John Dryden, by Jacques Maubert.

Rochester admired Dryden 'for the disproportion of him and his attributes'. Most portraits depict him with the distinguished air he wished for himself, but this one, despite the red plush, fine clothes, and distant view of Parnassus and Helicon, captures him as he was — troubled, troublesome, keen to appear fashionable, and somehow (despite his great poetic genius) demanding our pity. The dog seems to agree.

National Portrait Gallery, London.

complaisance of Cressida towards Diomede, whose misunderstanding by Troilus drives her to a satisfying suicide.

But to return to heroic tragedy. We have already dealt with its very real shortcomings. Its emotional evasions, and its frequent retreats into platitude or rhodomontade, compare badly with the scrupulous economy and terrifying intensity of Racine, who is exactly contemporary. Though frequently ornate, the verse has an air of being journalistically written, without pausing for the *mot juste*, without polishing and without pruning. But its appeal was genuine: in its verbal richness, its opportunity for spectacle, its confident heroicism (in an age whose battles did, after all, see spectacular gallantry), and, not least, its erotic charge. To modern audiences, who loathe rant, who will never see 'Mrs Ellen Guyn' or Mrs Marshal, and indeed are used to sex being far more freely discussed and performed on today's stages, these strong colours have faded. Yet it did have a rank theatricality, and a dignity too.

What was more, the Lady Brutes in the audience never needed to blow their noses. 'At Tragedies', says Sir Courtly Nice in Crowne's comedy of that name, 'the House is all lined with Beauty, and then a Gentleman may endure it.' And, though long stretches of dialogue seem machine-turned, with their far-fetched similes and their neatly symmetrical moral dilemmas, there are also some flashes of genuine poetry, such as Almahide's tears 'which silently each other's Track pursue', not to mention Aureng-Zebe's famous speech of despair in Act IV, surely the Restoration's closest equivalent to Hamlet's 'To be or not to be':

When I consider Life, 'tis all a Cheat;
Yet, fool'd with Hope, Men favour the Deceit;
Trust on, and think to-morrow will repay:
Tomorrow's falser than the former Day;
Lyes worse; and while it says, We shall be blest
With some new Joys, cuts off what we possest.
Strange Cozenage! none would live past Years
    again,
Yet all hope Pleasure in what yet remain;
And, from the Dregs of Life, think to receive
What the first sprightly Running could not
    give. . . .

The other side of the Restoration consciousness is beautifully expressed in Nourmahal's reply:

'Tis not for nothing that we Life pursue;
It pays our Hopes with something still that's
    new:
Each Day's a Mistress, unenjoy'd before;
Like travellers, we're pleas'd with seeing more.'

The plots of *Aureng-Zebe* and *Tyrannick Love* are a rich criss-cross of emotional attractions, divided loyalties, and shifts of power — less controlled than, say, Racine's *Andromaque*, but quite successful nevertheless. In *Tyrannick Love*, the Emperor Maximin's infatuation for Saint Catherine combines with the pursuit of his wife and his daughter respectively by two of his officers to make a drama of satisfying complexity. *Aureng-Zebe*, the most successful of the group, is set in Agra, a typically exotic locale producing the kind of deliberately evocative place names that Buckingham had matched with his 'Acton' and 'Putney'.

Even *The Conquest of Granada*, which is the weakest dramatically and relies largely on trumpets, drums, and the kind of

25. Dryden's *All for Love* in a modern revival.

James Laurenson as Antony and Diana Rigg as Cleopatra in the production at the Almeida Theatre, London, which opened in April 1991.

Ivan Kyncl and the Almeida Theatre.

heroic rant *The Rehearsal* parodies, boasts one magnificent character in the *seconda donna*, Lyndaraxa. Cast in the heroic-tragedy mould of the Irresistible Lady — invaluable as a plot device for motivating irrational action in the male characters — she spends the play's ten acts furiously pursuing the crown and unleashing sex-appeal on any man likely to help her to it. (Readers who have seen *All for Love* will recall that Cleopatra has a lot in common with her — but Dryden has too much respect for Cleopatra to represent her as truly coquettish, and has to motivate developments by more original means.) Her villainy and hypocrisy are delicious to watch, yet at the same time one pities her for being constantly frustrated in her sole desire.

When at last she is crowned Queen of Granada by the invading Spaniards, she hardly has time to draw breath before being fatally stabbed by one of her infuriated former lovers. Drawing herself upright, she claims that 'A Crown is come, and will not Fate allow', bawls that she will prosecute Death for treason, cries to the assembled Moors 'Bow down, ye Slaves', and in that moment of supreme satisfaction falls dead at their feet. Her vein of ironic melodrama, so close to comedy, is invincible in Dryden's hands. If it had ever been played by Sarah Bernhardt, it would have shaken the earth — not to mention the Académie's contempt for English tragedy.

All for Love (1677) is probably Dryden's best and most enduringly actable drama. It is not simply that his blank verse strives for, and achieves, a Shakespearean fluidity, economy, and closeness to speech; it is also that, very profitably, this play stands at a crossroads. Some of its power, notably in Cleopatra's death scene, is unashamedly borrowed from Shakespeare; the design's thrift and intensity certainly derives those qualities from Racine (*Phèdre* came out only a few months previously); yet much of the drama's vigour and irony — as well as its twists cleverly motivated by the evasions of an original character, the Queen's eunuch Alexa — are Dryden's and only his.

Dryden's poetic imagery in this play (as the critics have shown) lacks a centre, and his improvements on Shakespeare are unimpressive — notably his etiolated rewrite of 'The barge she sat in' — yet the whole has abundant dramatic vitality of a very special quality, as the stylish but energetic revival by Prospect Productions in 1977 showed. That production was rich in ironic laughter, which does bring the characters down to a more human level, most of all in the splendid scene of bitchery between Cleopatra and Octavia, who in Shakespeare never meet. Dryden put a great deal into this play, and could reasonably be contented with the result. It is the quintessence of tragedy in a refined age, yet a play which did not exclude genuine emotion as much as refinement would have liked.

Dryden claimed to find comedy difficult. His humour has a vitality equal to Wycherley's, which can hardly be feigned; but I think he never liked himself for being vulgar so successfully. His first comedy, *The Wild Gallant* (1663), is a crude, disorganised affair which only briefly comes to life when half the male characters are induced to believe they are suffering from pregnancy. But *Sir Martin Mar-All* (1667) — a tremendous success, attested by Pepys's enthusiasm and by references in other plays — is a splendid piece of fun, converting the charm and drollery of Molière's *L'Étourdi* into something wholly individual and British. By a stroke of genius, Dryden made Lélie, the young amorous twit who unerringly wrecks all plots made on his behalf, into the central character, a glorious noodle memorably impersonated by the great Nokes. The post-mortems that follow each and every occasion that Sir Martin promises not to put his foot in it, and then does so, develop into a sure-fire running gag. Pepys found it 'the most entire piece of mirth . . . the fullest of proper matter for mirth that ever was writ.'

The same year, 1667, also saw the appearance of *Secret Love*, called a tragi-comedy, but really a comedy combined with a romantic drama which is more intense, but without including deaths or battles and without breaking the characters' round of flirtations. Dryden increased its attractions by devising eight main female parts — for Mrs Marshal, Mrs Quin, Pepys's friend Mrs Knep, both the Mrs Davenports (one of whom, the great 'Roxolana', shortly left the stage for the Earl of Oxford), and his now-mistress Mrs Rutter. And the sixteen-year-old Nell Gwyn scored her first great success as the madcap girl Florimel, who, in her travesty scenes, makes the most sparkish of gallants. These last two plays, with *The Indian Emperour* (his own sequel to *The Indian Queen*), established him as the top-ranking playwright at a time when *Annus Mirabilis* made his reputation as a poet.

But his best comic writing comes in *Marriage à-la-Mode* (1672), whose quartet of lovers are given dialogue of a grace and brilliance unequalled in Restoration comedy. It is too bad that this is in fact a tragi-comedy, cursed with serious scenes sufficiently stodgy and absurd to render the whole work practically unactable. The exquisite flirtations of Rhodophil and Melantha, Palamede and Doralice, inhabit the fairy-tale world of *Love's Labour's Lost*, even if the soldierly Rhodophil, with his memorable turn of phrase, has a strong hint of Benedick:

Now Heav'n, of thy Mercy, bless me from this Tongue; it may keep the Field against a whole Army of Lawyers, and that in their own Language, French Gibberish. 'Tis true, in the day-time 'tis tolerable, when a Man has Field-room to run from it; but, to be shut up in a Bed with her, like two Cocks in a Pit; Humanity cannot support it: I must kiss all Night, in my own Defence, and hold her down, like a Boy at Cuffs, and give her the rising Blow every time she begins to speak.

In fact, she talks no more than he, and just as entertainingly:

In the Country! nay, that's to fall beneath the Town; for they live there upon our Offals here: Their Entertainment of Wit, is only the Remembrance of what they had when they were last in Town; they live this year upon the last Year's Knowledge, as their Cattel do all night, by chewing the Cud of what they eat in the Afternoon.

A far worse 'tongue' is owned by the outrageously affected Melantha, a female version of the 'Frenchified fop' who anticipates Vanbrugh's Lady Fancyfull in *The Provok'd Wife*. She learns a French

Dryden's *Marriage à-la-Mode* (1672) in two twentieth-century productions.

26. Lyric, Hammersmith, and Royalty Theatres, London, 1930:

a (left): Athene Seyler as Melantha with George Hayes as Palamede.

b (below). A passionately intense Glen Byam Shaw and Angela Baddeley as the serious lovers Leonidas and Palmyra.

Mander and Mitchenson Collection.

27. St James's Theatre, London, 1946.

a (right). Kay Hammond as Melantha.

b (below). Frances Rowe as Doralice parting Robert Eddison (Palamede) and John Clements (Rhodophil) in Act V.

c (next page). The comic climax of the tavern scene, as the two 'pages' (Melantha and Doralice) have to be forcibly restrained from attacking each other.

Mrs. Houston Rogers.

word-list daily to embellish her conversation ('Fourteen or fifteen words to serve me a whole Day! Let me die, at this rate I cannot last till Night . . .'), and then has the mirror held while she 'practises her Postures for the Day'. Erring husband and straying fiancé, each pursuing the other's lady, make assignations for the same grotto; the next night, both girls independently dress as pages, resulting in a rather frustrated *souper intime* for four at which the 'pages' argue incessantly; finally, Palamede conquers Melantha, blinding her with French and English at once. At first, it all seems no more than delicious nonsense, but its reflections on the marriage state, and its picture of human beings exploring their own emotions, are substantial enough:

I lov'd her [his wife] a whole half Year, double the natural Term of any Mistress, and think in my conscience I could have held out another Quarter, but then the World began to laugh at me, and a certain Shame of being out of Fashion, seiz'd me: At last, we arriv'd at that Point, that there was nothing left in us to make us new to one another. . . .

Such passages suggest that serious comedy would have been another genre Dryden might have adorned.

Dryden's single other great comedy, *The Kind Keeper, or Mr Limberham* (1678), is as different as anything could be. Where most Restoration comedies are set in the smartest parts of town, *Limberham* depicts goings-on in a second-rate boarding house. That, and the characters' cheerful, simple-minded lust, recalls Shadwell. In fact, it is the first bedroom farce of the English theatre, written with a spirit and freshness evident from the first page.

The surviving text of *Limberham* is not what was originally acted; but neither, as Dryden's preface emphasizes, is this a polished revision. What exactly happened is not clear, but it seems that the king, who had originally helped with the writing, banned the play after three nights, and that offending passages were altered or cut in the printed version. These alterations may substantially have marred the work, for the confusion in the later scenes is a sure sign of hasty patching and seaming. What caused the offence is equally obscure; like Ovid in a similar case, Dryden hardly dares hint. The pretext that it is licentious is unconvincing. (Its obsession with sex was curiously over-rated even at the time; one poet, Robert Gould, suggested that the script itself probably had the pox and needed medical treatment.) Maybe, as 'some Criticks in the Town' alleged, the pathetic character of Limberham, the 'tame, foolish keeper' in thrall to his kept mistress, was taken as personal satire by someone highly placed. Lauderdale (who had a notoriously determined mistress), Shaftesbury, even the Duke of York, have been suggested.

Possibly the character of Mrs Saintly, the sanctimonious landlady, unleashed on Dryden the fury that, a decade earlier, was to pursue *Tartuffe*. She is a masterly creation, whose religious language covers a multitude of sins from lechery ('I find a certain Motion within me to this young Man, and must secure him to my self, ere he see my Lodgers') to theft:

There is a certain Motion put into my Mind, and it is of good; I have Keys here, which a precious Brother, a devout Blacksmith, made me; and which will open any Lock of the same Bore: Verily, it can be no Sin to unlock this Chest therewith, and take from thence the spoils of the Ungodly. I will satisfy my conscience, by giving part thereof to the Hungry, and the Needy; some to our Pastor, that he may prove it lawful; and some I will sanctify to my own use.

In fact, the chest contains Woodall, the young hero, who threatens her with the eighth Commandment. Though religious 'enthusiasm' was certainly disapproved of in Restoration society, sustained ironic use of religious language was characteristic of Rochester and his friends at their most provocative — which could be too provocative, as Oxford Kate's showed.

Maybe, as Dryden suggests, he was a fool to venture such a farce at the height of the Popish Plot scare. But it is hard to see how any audience could resist the sparkling dialogue, or scenes like that in which Woodall is on a bed with one woman, finds another under the bed sticking needles into him with jealous fury, and is caught *in flagrante* by a third. Had we the *Limberham* that Dryden wrote, we might have a comic masterpiece instead of an entertaining near-miss.

The Popish Plot episode enlisted the pen of Dryden, as it did that of almost every important playwright. In fact, it produced *Absalom and Achitophel* and *The*

Medal — surely the most triumphant few years of his life. For the theatre, he wrote the controversial *Duke of Guise* with Nathaniel Lee, using episodes in French history of the sixteenth century which were uncannily parallel to Monmouth's current situation in asserting his right to the succession. This play, too, was suppressed, and the King's ban was only lifted at the end of 1682, when the tide had turned against Whig revolution, or the threat of it. Dryden's position was especially awkward, since his relations with Monmouth had always been warm. (This, indeed, is what gives the treatment of Absalom its peculiarly delicate quality.)

During James II's brief reign, following Dryden's conversion to Catholicism, he wrote *The Hind and the Panther*. When he returned to the stage in 1689, it was probably through lack of money as a deposed Laureate; but even these final, highly commercial plays and operas include a rich *Spätlese* in the shape of *Amphitryon* (1690), which remained popular long after his death.

Primarily, indeed, he was a commercial poet all along — which certainly accounts for his worst plays. At the height of the Dutch war in 1673 he produced *Amboyna, or The Cruelties of the Dutch Merchants against the English*, a claptrapping concoction of sadistic rape, torture, and jingoistic propaganda which would put Hollywood productions like *Vigilante Taskforce* in the shade. At the same time, his critical work, such as the *Essay of Dramatick Poesy*, exhibits an enquiring mind, a distinction alike of thought and language, which fully justifies his own opinion of himself. And, among Restoration playwrights, he comes closest to Shakespeare's versatility in every dramatic genre.

*

The problems of the following generation emerge clearly in the career of Thomas Otway. That career was brief: twenty years younger than Dryden, he produced his first play in 1675 at the age of twenty-three, and died only ten years later. By his death, he had written two tragedies which instituted yet another strain in Restoration drama — that of pathos. Though he had his successes, one of which (according to a lampoon) was notable for ridding him of lice and mange, Otway's life was a long losing battle against poverty, frustration, and despair. It provides a salutary commentary on a period which had no time for losers, and which has acquired a rosy glow in posterity's eyes by being largely described by, and in terms of, the winners.

Yet his promise was tremendous. What went wrong? 'A fine portly graceful Man' is Oldys's arresting description, 'of a middle size, about 5 foot 7 inches, inclinable to Corpulancy, but a thoughtful yet lively and as it were speaking Eye.' His sensitivity as a person is fully displayed in his work: 'The passions, in the raising of which, he had a Felicity peculiar to himself', said Tom Brown, 'are represented in such lively Colours that they cannot fail of affecting the most insensible Hearts with pleasing Agitations.' The 'pleasing Agitations' set the scene for the eighteenth century's theatre of sentiment. No-one wept at the death of Dryden's Jocasta, but the tears raised by Otway and his actors (notably Mrs Barry, who knew how to stir emotions) ensured his popularity for a

28. Thomas Otway: Soest.

One of Buckhurst's portraits from Knole, capturing the poet's plump good looks and his curious brooding quality.

Knole.

century and a half. Sheridan's Tilburina, stark mad in white satin, is clearly the last of a line that starts with Otway's picturesquely insane Belvidera —

Murmuring streams, soft shades, and spring-
*   ing flowers,*
Lutes, Laurells, Seas of Milk, and ships of
*   Amber. . . .*
The Winds! hark how they whistle!
And the Rain beats: oh how the weather
*   shrinks me!*

— and ends with the theatrically pathetic griefs and lunacies of Donizetti's Lucia and Anna Bolena. 'More tears have been shed, probably, for the sorrows of Belvidera [*Venice Preserv'd*] and Monimia [*The Orphan*] than for those of Juliet and Desdemona': thus Sir Walter Scott, as late as 1819.

Don Carlos, produced in 1676 when he was twenty-four, was Otway's first great success. In his Preface appears all his excitement at acceptance in the literary world, with some cocky hits at Dryden, who had been ungenerous, and an amusing account of his work:

I must confess I had often a Titillation to
Poetry, but never durst venture on my Muse,
till I got her into a corner in the Country, and
then like a bashful young Lover when I had her
private I had courage to fumble, but never
thought she would have produc'd any thing,
till at last I know not how, e're I was aware,
I found my self Father of a Dramatique
birth. . . .

This engagingly licentious description makes a poignant contrast with the fruitless toil that work and the pursuit of love

later became. Very soon he was sucked into the vortex of literary backbiting, treachery, and cheap satire. As we have seen, his friendly relationship with Rochester broke up. He spent a year on military service in Flanders, which brought him back to London, unpaid except for worthless debentures. *The Souldiers Fortune* (1680), a light but eminently actable comedy (as Peter Gill's spirited Royal Court production proved in 1967), describes the amorous adventures of two such embittered demobs.

Otway's two most characteristic tragedies, *The Orphan* (1680) and *Venice Preserv'd* (1682), were both well received, but in 1685 he died as poor as ever — according to one account, choking on his first crust for days. Perhaps, crippled by depression, he simply did not produce enough — profits even on a success did not sustain a writer long, and Dryden and Shadwell wrote a great deal more. It is known that he took to drink, which his hopeless affair with Mrs Barry can only have aggravated.

We cannot refuse our sympathy; his heart is so near the surface. Even in the Epilogue to the light-hearted *Souldiers Fortune* he describes how

With the discharge of Passions much opprest,
Disturb'd in Brain, and pensive in his Breast,
Full of those thoughts which make th'unhappy
*   sad,*
And by Imagination half grown mad,
The Poet led abroad his Mourning Muse,
And let her range, to see what sport she'd
*   chuse.*
Strait like a bird got loose, and on the Wing,
Pleas'd with her freedom, she began to Sing,
'Wretch, write no more for an uncertain fame.'

29. Anthony Ashley Cooper, first Earl of Shaftesbury, after John Greenhill.

A typically penetrating portrait of the original for Antonio in Venice Preserv'd, *and hated butt of most dramatists towards the end of Charles II's reign.*

National Portrait Gallery, London.

Imagine this recited to a pitful of peri-wigs. Otway was not afraid to tell the *beau monde* that he suffered — which was endearing, but neither well-bred nor wise. Perhaps the *larmoyant* strain in English literature has not been an unmixed bless-ing, but Otway's public enjoyed it, and his miserable death is a blot on the period.

Remarkably, all his plays, tragic and comic, revert to the same obsessions — the grievances of the malcontent (a uniquely anguished figure in Otway, quite unlike Jacobean drama's scheming malevolents) and the sexual jealousy of young have-nots towards elderly haves. The latter, of course, is a startling reversal of the Res-toration comedy norm as exemplified in *The Country Wife*, and indicates a defeatist mentality that went deep in Otway. Ex-amples are frequent and various, from the brisk cuckolding of Sir Davy Dunce in *The Souldiers Fortune* to the violent jealousy of Pierre in *Venice Preserv'd*, who knows his mistress is being bought by the disgusting old senator Antonio.

While Otway's plays can hardly be considered in detail here, some sign-posting is essential. For one thing, his 'sportive Muse' has never been fully appreciated. *The Souldiers Fortune* and *Friendship in Fashion* have at times a bitter-ness which looks backward to Wycherley and forward to Congreve's sour little essay on human relations, *The Double Dealer* (1693). Some of his comedy is full of subtle half-lights. The Nurse in *Caius Marius* (1679), his reworking of *Romeo and Juliet*, describes Juliet in cleverly managed terms which combine innocent pathos with sustained *double entendre*: 'When it was a Little thing, and us'd to ly with me, it wou'd so kick, so sprawl, and so play . . .

and then I would tickle it, and then it would laugh, and then it would play agen. When it had tickling and playing enough, it would go to sleep as gently as a Lamb. I shall never forget it . . .'. On finding her babe dead to the world, she exclaims 'I will sigh, and cry till I am swell'd as big as a Pumkin.'

Otway's great early tragedy, *Don Carlos*, shows a comic skill: the soliloquies of King Philip, Eboli, Don John of Austria, or Ruy-Gomez usually reveal, after some highly emotional scene, that they have actually been double-crossing Carlos, Posa, the Queen, or each other. This irony brings an agreeably Jacobean tartness to a fascin-ating play. The hero, as any lover of Verdi's opera will recognise, fits perfectly into the Otwavian mould of deprivation and passionate frustration. In fact, the play would still be very actable but for a grotesque ending with multiple deaths and a King Philip who, after uttering some highly improbable heroic verse, 'runs off raving'.

The Orphan, though very important in its time, is nothing but an implausible tearjerker. Mrs Barry *did* move tears when she cried out into the night and sum-moned the wrong lover to her bed. But if, as several critics have felt, *Romeo and Juliet* makes one feel that the characters have just had very bad luck, *The Orphan* forces one to conclude that they had rotten eye-sight as well.

Otway's last tragedy, *Venice Preserv'd*, is a *tour de force*, which will still hold the stage whenever its formidable emotional demands can be sustained by cast and audience. Here are the Otwavian malcon-tents in their most haunting form — the passionately idealistic Jaffeir and Pierre,

30. A rare revival of Otway's *The Souldiers Fortune.*

Peter Gill's 1967 production for the English Stage Company at the Royal Court.

Douglas Jeffery and the Theatre Museum.

seeking by revolution to rid the state of Venice from the dominance of the old, worn out, and corrupt. But, curiously, they nowhere indulge in abstract-filled rhetoric about their actions; rather, Otway makes it plain that, however morally reprehensible their enemies, Jaffeir and Pierre are principally motivated by their failure and frustration in society. Otway's analysis of the revolutionary impulse is the same as Cicero's, envy and deprivation, making *Venice Preserv'd* a personal, psychological tragedy: passionate but lacking in breadth.

The audience's sympathy is enlisted, not by admiration for their patriotism (a commonplace from, say, Goethe's *Egmont* onwards), but by pity and admiration for their heroism and loyalty. Their plot has a desperation from the start which dooms it to failure if the audience has a sixth sense. But it's precisely this desperation, this feverish romanticism that almost welcomes disaster as wife or companion is embraced for the last time, that gives *Venice Preserv'd* its power. It has to be performed at fever pitch throughout, which for modern actors demands as much courage, perhaps foolhardiness, as the characters they portray. Or perhaps, as Sir John Gielgud (himself a brilliantly successful Jaffeir) has suggested, it is the first of the great melodramas, written with great sincerity and strength and designed to be so played.

Finally, *Venice Preserv'd* is notable for the period's most vivid and vicious dramatic caricature. Into the figure of Antonio, the lecherous old goat of a senator who pesters Pierre's mistress Aquilina, Otway pours his hatred of corrupt old age in office and his most committed Tory sentiments. For Antonio, who describes himself in Act III, Scene i, as being sixty-one years old, is Anthony Ashley Cooper, Earl of Shaftesbury — the leading Whig minister for much of the reign, the King's *bête noire*, and the most calculating exploiter of 'Popish Plot' hysteria, which had just passed its peak when *Venice Preserv'd* was produced. Veiled references to the Plot are frequent in this conspiracy play, but the Antonio scenes themselves have an independent dramatic life — comic, satirical, and perhaps more disgusting than either.

Antonio addresses his mistress in an endless drivel of pet-names like Nicky-Nacky, and invites her to play games in which sado-masochism is only tempered by the eccentricity of dotage. And the poverty-stricken Otway, fresh from writing desperate letters to a woman who 'should you ley with her all night . . . would not know you next Morning, unless you had another five Pounds at her Service', makes money's purchasing power abundantly clear when Antonio punctuates his speeches with repeated shakes of his purse.

*

Thomas Shadwell, by contrast, was easy-going and a stayer. Of all Restoration comedies, it is his garrulous, cheerful, untidy works that most recall the Jacobeans. When we read a speech like 'There's none so bad as thee, old Puss. Thou filthy, toothless, wormeaten old Maid, I'll maul thee, thou witch of *Endor*', we begin to think we are reading Ben Jonson (as we have seen, his most famous character, Sir Positive At-All, has a distinctly Jonsonian ring). Every page abounds with such mouthfilling delights; yet frequently the whole is so disorganised that modern directors might well despair of cutting them into any coherence.

Le style, c'est l'homme lui-même. Shadwell's most famous pen-portrait comes from an arch-enemy:

Now stop your noses Readers, all and some,
For here's a turn of Midnight-work to come,
Og *from a Treason-Tavern rolling home.*
Round as a Globe, and Liquor'd every chink,
Goodly and Great he Sails behind his Link.
With all this bulk there's nothing lost in Og,
For ev'ry inch that is not Fool is Rogue. . . .

Shadwell, genial as he was, would hardly have complained at this. It was not so far from Shadwell as Shadwell saw himself. He drank wine with Otway, ale with Buckhurst and the actor Harris — and, in fact, one envies them. 'The Wit of his Conversation was often very Immoral Obscene and Profane', says Oldys; while Rochester remarked that Shadwell should have burnt his writings and printed his talk.

The 'Treason Tavern' of Dryden's squib is, of course, significant; Shadwell was one of the Whig pamphleteers, whom Dryden thought disgustingly venal as well as dangerous — even if, as was alleged, he paid the King enough in claret tax to outweigh his anti-royalist scribblings. As one of Shaftesbury's journalistic crew, he naturally figures in *Absalom and Achitophel*. When Dryden wrote the Tory *Duke of Guise*, Shadwell reacted as swiftly and voluminously as both of them, in conjunction, had against the loathed Settle eight years earlier. The weapons, the style of humour, the contemptuous nit-picking, were the same; today's friend was tomorrow's enemy and *vice versa*, but the political rift between Dryden and Shadwell endured. This is the background to that moment in 1689, so bitter to Dryden, when Shadwell's mottled and unpretentious brows received the royal laurel.

The Sullen Lovers (1668) was his first play and an enormous success, but apart from Sir Positive it is a miserable morass of verbosity and endlessly repeated situations. Like so many of his plays, it starts from a Molière original, to which Shadwell referred in scathing terms. But the best of his scenes and characters are full of vitality, even if he does milk them for every passing moment without much thought for building effects. One soon learns not to expect dramatic economy, but its absence remains irritating.

His uproarious satire once again recalls Jonson. *The Virtuoso* (1676) guys the scientific speculations of the new Royal Society just as Jonson had ridiculed alchemy. Sir Nicholas Gimcrack learns to swim by lying on a table and imitating a frog — he scorns practical experiments — and puts a sheep's blood into a man with gratifyingly ovine results ('He calls himself the meanest of my Flock, and sent me some of his own Wooll'). Using putrid flesh as a source of light ('I my self have read a *Geneva* Bible by a Leg of Pork') remains wonderfully absurd, but, unwit-

31. Thomas Shadwell: an early eighteenth-century engraving.

The frontispiece to his 1720 complete works, taken from his memorial in Westminster Abbey, shows Shadwell complacent with alcoholic serenity beneath the Poet Laureate's wreath. Tom Brown's Latin epitaph for him neatly inverted a cliché by bidding earth lie heavy on him, since he had lain heavy on earth. His English epitaph was more affectionate:

And must our glorious Laureat then depart!
Heav'n, if it please, may take his loyal Heart;
As for the rest, sweet devil, fetch a Cart.

tingly, some of the other satire has rebounded with the progress of knowledge. Witness Sir Nicholas's description of the Moon:

'Tis as big as our Earth; I can see all the

32. *The Virtuoso* revived: scenes from Peter Duguid's production for Thames Television, 1975.

a (above). Sir Nicholas Gimcrack learns to swim 'theoretically'.

b (opposite page). Women of wit pursued by witty men: Dinsdale Landen and Chris Jarvis as the heroes, Jacqueline Tony as Miranda, Mollie Sugden as Lady Gimcrack, and Hazel Copper as Mrs Figgup.

Thames Television.

Mountainous Parts, and Vallies, and Seas, and Lakes in it; nay, the larger Sort of Animals, as Elephants and Camels; but publick Buildings and Ships very easily. . . .

In fact, as two American scholars, C. S. Duncan and A. S. Borgman, have shown, all these examples derive from actual scientific experiments of the time, seized on by Shadwell from reports in the transactions of the Royal Society itself.

But, you ask, how can these amazing *obiter dicta* ever crop up in a play with a plot? How indeed. There seem to be half-a-dozen plots going on simultaneously, all used from hand to mouth. But it is useless to look in Shadwell for what is not there. Instead we should try to enjoy his real strength: character-drawing of unweariable liveliness and variety, and the dialogue to go with it. Like Ben Jonson, he enjoys the full range of humankind at all levels of society, and is the only Restoration comic writer to move with sustained success outside fashionable London — as witness his bourgeois intrigues at Epsom, rustic superstitions in Lancashire, or that supremely Jonsonian picture of the underworld and its rich *argot* in *The Squire of Alsatia* (1688).

Sometimes, as in *A True Widow* (1678), he directs his satire very close to home. *A True Widow* is almost a seventeenth-century *Otherwise Engaged*, surrounding the reasonable heroes with a throng of sharply differentiated types of relentless, infuriating affectation. Mr Selfish, combing his peruke while describing his mouthwatering conquests ('There is a pretty Creature, not past Eighteen, whom I have formerly enjoy'd. . . . I have had three Maidenheads this week'), or Young Maggot, doubling him in hearts ('I had a Billet from the prettiest Creature of Sixteen to Day, I'll tell you . . .') — these two can still be heard in present-day London, straight and gay, hysterically asserting their claims to envy. So, if we look in the right places, can Prig, the horsey type rambling off reams of his studfarm genealogies:

I am come to get you to look upon the best bred Horse in England; Woodcock *was his Grandfather; he is the Son of* Bay-lusty, *and the Brother of* Red-rose; *his Sister is the*

33. *Epsom Wells* at the Thorndike Theatre, Leatherhead, 1969.

A Shadwell character in full spate: Mrs Jilt, 'a silly affected Whore', attempts to endear herself to Clodpate by disparaging London for a 'nasty, stinking, wicked Town'. Josephine Tewson and Robert Cartland in Anthony Wiles's production.

Frank Page Studios.

White-mare, *the cousin German of* Crack-a-Fart; *Cousin once removed to* Nutmeg; *third Cousin to my Lord* Squander's *Colt; ally'd to* Flea-bitten *by the second Venture. . . .*

No wonder Prig provided Regency theatre with its favourite cliché character — and

even the co-heroine Isabella is furnished with a modern type of a sister in Gartrude, 'very foolish and whorish', who is anybody's so long as he has the brightest buttons, the blondest periwig, the fastest patter.

At the centre of *A True Widow*, however, as of almost all Shadwell's plays, are the two couples: two ladies of wit, beauty, and means courted by two similar gentlemen. These characters are Shadwell's heaviest compliment to his aristocratic patrons in the audience. Many of those were, in fact, Selfishes and Maggots and Prigs; still others resembled the pox-ridden, debt-ridden, vanity-ridden Crazy, whose cracked-up body is such a brilliantly exploited source of entertainment in *The Humourists* (1670), or the snobbish, conceited Sir Timothy in *The Lancashire Witches* (1681). But they saw themselves as Longvil and Bruce, Raymund, Lovel and Carlos, 'Gentlemen of Wit and Sense'.

We know, at least, that Buckhurst and Buckingham and Rochester and Sedley *did* endear themselves to writers by their frankness, openness, and sense of proportion; in fact, Oldys and Buckingham imply that their contributions to Shadwell's plays were very substantial. So those playwrights simply had to overlook the times when they ran amuck.

In short, Shadwell's picture of society betrays the restrictions, in practice, on his own freedom of speech. Did Buckhurst never let a smug boast pass his lips when the sixteen-year-old town sensation went to live with him? *A True Widow* is actually dedicated to Sedley; but a glance at Sedley's plays makes Shadwell's eulogies of his wit seem grossly unconvincing.

ACT FOUR
Four Craftsmen and One Woman

OUR LAST clutch of playwrights are minor, but have an interest of their own. Judged on his best plays, in fact, John Crowne is not a minor writer, but his work is very uneven. We met him earlier as Rochester's protégé, graciously embarrassed at being chosen to write a Court masque over the head of Dryden. He seems to have been sensitive, shy, rather an exquisite, but very independent. His best-known comedy, *Sir Courtly Nice* (1685), draws its most successful effects from the contrast between the fastidious Sir Courtly (an amiable caricature of the author), who sends his laundry to Holland and gave up drinking wine when he saw the treaders' feet, and the belching, swearing and grossly demonstrative Surly. (This of course anticipates Congreve's Witwoud and Sir Wilfull.) As we have seen, the early scenes were written under the King's supervision.

But as good or better is his earlier play *The Countrey Wit* (1675), a thoroughly lovable comedy which manages to unite some widely different sources of fun into a genial and satisfying whole. The incorrigibly roving hero Ramble; his quietly faithful lover Christina and her mischievously witty sister, the fantastical Lady Faddle; the bickering of Lord Drybone and his rebellious mistress Betty; and the Country Wit himself, Sir Mannerly Shallow, with his man Booby in tow — all these keep their humours and their separate corners of the plot on the boil throughout.

Sir Mannerly, who hopes to marry Christina, goes through the show mistaking her porter for her lordly father and honouring him accordingly. With equal optimism, Lady Faddle pursues Ramble:

The Top, the Cream, the Flower, the Quintessence, of Wit and Ingenuity; his harmonious Tongue has left a tang, a relish of a Passion behind it; I swear, I feel a little Palpitation, I shall not be at repose, till I commence my Intrigue; and oh my brutish and obtuse memory, I have forgot to ask him, what happy place he honours with his abode. . . .

Ramble, meanwhile, is attracted by Betty. And all the plots come together in one magnificent ensemble: the porter prepares to palm his daughter off as Christina, Ramble threatens Sir Mannerly while his servant Merry distracts Bobby with tales of an ox-race for hay 'to be eat all with Mustard . . . and the Ox that wins, to be Knighted', and a beggar woman, who has hitherto seemed superfluous, suddenly swaps her brat for Booby's moneybag, leaving him literally holding the baby and exposed to the foulest accusations.

Crowne's comic style, at its best, yields the palm to nobody. Laura's great speech from Act III, Scene ii, of *The English Friar* (1690), an unusually sustained flight of fancy, would make a perfect audition piece for a young actress seeking something unfamiliar:

What shou'd we mind else, dear Sister, whilst we have any share of youth and beauty? I do love Love. I wou'd have all the Love i' the World; and I have good store, when I go to Court all eyes are upon me, all tongues are whispring that's my Lord Statelys *fine Daughter; all press towards me and bow, only to get half a glance from me. When I go to the Plays, the Minute I appear, the whole Pit turns round as mov'd by an Engine; to please themselves with the sight of me, the most entertaining Scene in the House. Some stand gazing on me, with their arms a cross, their heads languishing as opprest with Beauty. The brisker fellows fall a whetting their Arrows presently, that is, Comb their Wigs, and prepare their eyes to tilt with mine. When I go to* Hide *Park, my motions seem to turn the World, for, as I turn, all the Coaches i' the Circle turn to meet mine. The Ladies to see my Dresses, the men to see me. There do I ride i' my shining Chariot, like the Moon on a bright Cloud, while all the little beautys move round beneath me, like Fairys.*

Ironically, one of Crowne's greatest successes was *The Destruction of Jerusalem by Titus Vespasian* (1677), a two-part work on the lines of Dryden's *Conquest of Granada*, but relying heavily on sensational spectacle (the burning of the Temple on stage is one of Drury Lane's first examples of scenic extravagance in what later became the Augustus Harris style), and conspicuously lacking Dryden's ease with powerful, flexible heroic verse.

Its success is said to have robbed Crowne of the friendship of Rochester; all the more regrettable, then, that there is no record of Rochester's reaction to *The Ambitious Statesman* (1679), which Crowne knew was his finest work and is in fact one of the greatest Restoration tragedies. It is a grippingly plotted and impressively written study of court psychology and court intrigue under Charles VI of France, and into it Crowne poured all his hatred of court society, for which he had a 'Mortal Aversion' even when he was in favour. He also refused to 'make court to multitudes, and therefore they never did, or will make court to me', he complained. Both ways he ensured the play's failure, especially at a time of the intensest political unrest.

But Rochester, already in his last and blackest phase, would have been proud to write it. Crowne was never to touch such heights in tragedy again. Perhaps, like Congreve, he abdicated after the failure of his masterpiece, and did not venture to load such an accident-prone medium with any more really precious ideas.

Crowne's blank verse in *The Ambitious Statesman* has a swiftness and style that make one wonder how he can have perpetrated the stilted, predictable couplets of *Jerusalem*. Consider the compact expression and powerful bitterness of this, from the second act:

Wars are good Physick when the World is sick.
But he who cuts the Throats of Men for glory,
Is a vain savage Fool; he strives to build

Immortal Honours upon man's mortality,
And glory on the shame of humane Nature,
To prove himself a man by Inhumanity.
He puts whole Kingdoms in a blaze of War,
Only to still Mankind into a Vapour;
Empties the World to fill an idle Story.
In short, I know not why he shou'd be
　　honour'd,
And they that murder men for money hang'd.

Or the Shakespearean ring of this, from Act III:

'Tis very natural vain things shou'd be
　　uppermost,
In such a World of Vanity as this;
Where massy substances of things sink down,
And nothing stays but Colours, Sounds, and
　　Shadows.
What mighty things derive their power from
　　Colours:
Courts owe their Majesty to Pomp, and
　　Shew:
Altars their Adoration, to their Ornaments:
Women their Lovers, to their Paint and
　　Washes;
Fools their esteem to Perewigs and Ribbons.
How many Trades are there that live by
　　tones?
The cheating Beggar whines our Money from
　　us;
The Player by his tone will make us weep,
When Men's substantial sorrows cannot do it.
An Orator will set the World a dancing
After his pipe when Reason cannot stir it.
Fanatick canting Priests, will o'erturn
　　Kingdoms
Only by tones, and thumping upon Pulpits.
And silly human heards, as soon as e're
They hear the wooden thunder, prick up Ears,
And Tails, and frighted run they know not
　　whither.

The first speech is a refreshing reaction from the raving war-heroes of Dryden and Settle — Almanzor and the rest — while the second moves imperceptibly from general Jacobean melancholy to a strong implied attack on the whipped-up anti-Papist frenzy which suspended the rule of law in the London of 1679.

It is no accident that both come, not from the mouth of the Constable of France, the dangerous malcontent of the play's title, but from the hero, his son the Duke. Introduced as a 'studious, moral fool', the Duke immediately commands our interest. He is, in fact, an unusually sympathetic figure combining the philosophical and intellectual gifts of Hamlet, the military *virtù* of Fortinbras, and an unswerving integrity which is all his own — and which arouses his father's hatred. Set up by him as a rebel, tortured by the Dauphin, he turns the tables on his father by using the success of his party of 'rebels' only to restore the royal power, and then dies in great style beside the lady of whom, once again, his father's machinations have robbed him:

May I have leave, Sir, —
To sleep in Death by her who was your
　　Princess?
But in the Grave there's no Propriety,
In Death's dark ruinous Empire all lyes
　　waste. . . .
Then come cold Bride to my as cold
　　Embrace!
The Grave's our Bed, and Death our Bridal-
　　Night,
None will disturb, or envy our Delight.

On that sardonic note, this remarkable hero passes from our view.

Elkanah Settle ('Phoebus, what a name!', as Byron would certainly have said) is that figure without which no period of theatre history would be complete — the whizz-kid. Like his successors, he may even have had a play produced while he was still at Oxford. Whatever its date, *Cambyses* is a remarkable piece of work, far too complicated (there are ten principal characters, all loving, fighting, and plotting like fury) but dramatically ingenious. Certainly at an early age he acquired a privileged popularity with court and town that brought upon him the jealousy of most established authors.

His greatest success was *The Empress of Morocco*, not necessarily a better play than *Cambyses*, but one which came to the Duke's theatre after two productions at court (with casts of 'great personages', and prologues by Mulgrave and Rochester respectively) had made it fashionable. It was published (in 1673 — probably after only a few months) with illustrations that provide valuable information about the contemporary theatre, and went through two impressions almost at once.

Like Lee, Settle specialised in romantic writing, and laid himself wide open to criticisms of his irrational imagery, defective sense, and incorrect versifying — much like those which, a century and a half later, Macaulay in the *Edinburgh Review* heaped on the egregious Robert Montgomery. Settle versus the rest (with Dryden, Crowne, and Shadwell in the van) became one of the period's classic literary squabbles, which, as so many did, combined private envy with a very serious technical controversy — in this case the old chestnut of blank verse against the heroic couplet — on which Dryden's feelings were already

changing. (Note that this is 1674 — practically the last date at which one will find Dryden on the same side as either Shadwell or Crowne.

Dryden's hatred of Settle remained something special — intensifying when he joined Shadwell and the Whigs during the crisis of 1678-82, devising Pope-burning pageants and writing an attack on *Absalom and Achitophel*. Unbelievably, on James II's accession Settle turned Tory, and he and Dryden, newly converted Catholic, found themselves on the same side. After James was expelled, Settle attempted to retain favour by writing a eulogy of William III, but achieved little except an appointment as 'city Poet' in charge of pageants. He probably adapted *A Midsummer Night's Dream* for Purcell's *Fairy Queen* in 1692, and later still appeared as a dragon (in a green costume 'of his own invention') in a show at Bartholomew Fair.

No question but Settle was lucky, as other poets had not been, in achieving runaway success with an unexceptional play; but *The Empress of Morocco* is not as contemptible as they liked to suggest, and their nit-picking, though entertaining in small quantities (as nit-picking often is), does them little credit. Settle's plotting is sometimes fiendishly effective, as in the famous scene when the young heroine, disguised as Eurydice, is cheated into stabbing Orpheus (actually her own lover) at a masquerade, and some equally celebrated lines like

Then with his dying Breath his Soul retir'd
And in a sullen sigh his Life expir'd

do pungently express their purposed meaning — here the flight of the basic

34. Elkanah Settle's *The Empress of Morocco*: a contemporary engraving.

The opening scene at the Duke of York's playhouse, 1673, showing Muly Labas and Morena dressed as an unashamedly Restoration couple.

Christopher Baugh.

personality ('Soul') and resultant sense of hopeless defeat in the poisoned King. (The rival poets miss all this: 'That is, just as he dyed, he dyed, and when he dyed his soul expired, his life retired, and he dyed.') And, though some of Settle's lines are at least as absurd as Dryden's worst, or Lee's, he has no difficulty, in a surprisingly well-mannered pamphlet, in throwing out accusations to match the ones he cannot parry. One could forgive him much for the diverting passage in which he maintains that Dryden, the arch-plagiarist, had actually borrowed from his own Martin Mar-All to make the tragic hero Almanzor.

*

Nathaniel Lee's tragedies are better known, though not entirely with justice. As Professor Roswell Ham showed in a unique double biography, Lee's career makes a remarkable parallel with Otway's, moving from their early success and high creative energy to disillusion, sterility, poverty, and, in Lee's case, madness. He certainly possessed dramatic skill, and his plays always promise to be interesting, but never quite are. He misses the unexpected master-stroke of plot or character (in fact, his accomplished poetry conceals some positively cardboard characterisation), he makes little use of humour, and his real stock-in-trade, practised without cynicism, is highly-coloured rhetoric and the lurid *coup de théâtre,* such as decks out his *Oedipus* (1678) with fantastical portents and finally obliges the blinded hero to leap out of a window.

There is every indication, though, that Lee felt and believed in his own feverish

poetic experience, however consciously baroque it can sometimes seem. Oldys gives an endearing picture of 'Nat' reading his scripts to the cast, his 'harmonious voice' and expressive interpretation putting the professionals to shame; and, of course, there is his final lunacy to testify that his poetic eccentricities were not assumed with an eye to 'conscious bewilderment of the poetic faculties'.

But even in his own tolerant day, it was noticed that much of his writing was little better than senseless rant. His *Alexander the Great* (1677) was enormously popular, but only a really great actor like Betterton or Mountfort could get away with it. And when one of the rival heroines raves like this in Act III, do we call it pretentious rubbish or the vagaries of a mind unable to keep its bounds?

Roxana *and* Statira, *they are Names*
That must for ever jar; eternal Discord,
Fury, Revenge, Disdain, and Indignation
Tear my swoll'n Breast, make way for Fire and
   Tempest.
My Brain is burst, Debate and reason
   quench'd
The Storm is up, and my hot bleeding Heart
Splits with the Rack, while Passions like the
   Winds,
Rise up to Heaven, and put out all the Stars.

Testimonies to Lee's sweetness of nature are frequent. Even Dryden was happy to work with him. In Bedlam he attracted many visitors, not all come to laugh. During semi-lucid intervals he planned to write ever more grandiose plays, or moaned the loss of his fine hair, cut off in the customary manner. Perhaps he even remembered his prophetic description in *Caesar Borgia*:

Look a poor Lunatick that makes his Moan,
And for a time beguiles the Lookers on,
He reasons well, his Eyes their Wildness lose,
And vows his Keepers his wrong'd Sense
  abuse:
But if you hit the Cause that hurts his Brain,
Then his Teeth gnash, he foams, he shakes his
  Chain,
His Eye-balls roll, and he is mad again.

*

Edward Ravenscroft, originally a Middle Temple lawyer, was one of those hacks without whom the theatres' ravenous demand for new plays could never have been satisfied. He rose to success in 1672 with an adaptation of Molière's *Le Bourgeois Gentilhomme* which drove rival authors to despair with its crude but effective 'Mamamouchi' charades, and proceeded to pilfer from Spanish, French, and Italian originals ad lib for a succession of mostly rather indecent potboiler farces, few of which have ever been re-published.

Yet in 1681, the period of the Popish Plot, stimulated by the Town's anti-City and anti-Shaftesbury animus, Ravenscroft raised prejudice to comic delight in one supremely inspired comedy, *The London Cuckolds*, which held the stage for a hundred years and was traditionally performed every Lord Mayor's Day, just to keep the City in its place. Well constructed and amusingly written, with a strengthening hint of the universal in its characters, it became probably the most unjustly neglected Restoration comedy, until its revival at the Lyric, Hammersmith, in 1985.

The keynote is quickly established: resentment by the heroes, and by implication the audience, of old City whigs, who are 'petitioning' for the Duke of York's exclusion from the succession. And, as in Otway's contemporary piece *The Souldiers Fortune*, resentment suggests revenge:

TOWNLY. *What is her husband?*
RAMBLE. *A blockheaded City attorney; a trudging, drudging, cormudging, petitioning citizen, that with a little law and much knavery has got a great estate.*
TOWNLY. *A petitioner! Cuckold the rogue for that very reason.*

There follows an uproariously farcical series of adventures, with some near misses, some furious disappointments, and not a few delicious conquests. Townly and Ramble are a pair of likely lads, beautifully contrasted; Ramble tries really hard for his pleasures and always misses, Townly never tries yet always succeeds. For much of the play Ravenscroft plays one against the other, with Ramble shut out, or even stuck half-out of the window, while his mistress unwittingly summons Townly's equally congenial embraces.

A note of true emotion is lightly struck by Loveday, the true lover of one of the aldermen's young wives, who manages to enjoy her but must relinquish her in the end. Arabella, the other (one of Mrs Barry's great comic roles), shines in a memorable scene with her admirer in which, while keeping her promise to her husband to say 'No' to every question, she still contrives to be very expressive.

*

Women dramatists remain rare, even today, and Aphra Behn probably remains the most prolific and (with the rather

35. Mrs Aphra Behn, by Sir Peter Lely.

Shown here as buoyant, independent, and as attractive as one of her own heroines.

Hulton Picture Library.

special exception of Agatha Christie) successful in theatre history. Her unusually plucky personality packed her life to the full, both as an author and as a human being. Daughter of a colonial administrator posted to the West Indies (which gave her first-hand material for *Oroonoko*, the first of her highly successful novelettes), she early married a Dutch merchant and, on his death, was left at the age of twenty-four to fend for herself. She chose to do some valuable spying for England under the code-name of 'Astraea' — which stuck. Like Dryden, also a royal servant, she found late payment for her activities a serious difficulty — in fact, she ended up in prison for debt. From then on, her struggles were acute, and her war became that of meeting a man's world on its own terms.

Apart from the novels, Aphra Behn wrote approximately twenty plays, mostly comedies, between 1670 and her death in 1689 at the age of forty-nine. Their character graphically expresses what we know of her personality: abundant vitality, a facility with words, good humour (she was the kindest of hostesses and, it is said, invented milk punch), and a racy imagination. She had a reputation for writing bawdy — 'Astraea', wrote Pope, 'fairly puts all characters to bed'. But perhaps it would be truer to say that she had a facility for putting herself into the minds of both sexes when pleasure-bent.

Aptly enough, one of her plays is dedicated to Nell Gwyn, in terms which both ladies must have enjoyed seeing through:

I make this Sacrifice with infinite fear and trembling, well knowing that so Excellent and perfect a Creature as your self differs only from the Divine powers in this: the Offerings made to you ought to be worthy of you, whilst they accept the will alone.

But, equally, a genuine appreciation shines through:

You never appear but you glad the hearts of all that have the happy fortune to see you, as if you were made on purpose to put the whole world into good Humour.... And so well you bear the honours you were born for, with a greatness so unaffected, an affability so easie, an Humour so soft, so far from Pride or Vanity, that the most Envious and most disaffected can finde no cause or reason to wish you less, Nor can Heaven give you more....

Posterity saw Aphra Behn as a luscious, vital lady who drank deep of pleasure; and, though her life, more often, was a scribbler's struggle as bad as Dryden's, that was not far from the character she identified with and admired. Her plays do lack discipline in both dialogue and plotting; their vivacity often descends to a garrulousness which would make modern directors fling them out in despair; and, though she takes enthusiastically to the Spanish and Italian settings of her plots, one only has to look at Shadwell's comparable effort (*The Amorous Bigot* of 1690, a really delightful piece) to see how she lacked dramatic invention. Yet her work is a picture of herself; and one admires her.

Her likeness was uncannily caught, fifty years after her death, by a writer who can barely have known her, fancifully describing her vain attempts, as a ghost, to enter Poets' Corner:

36. *The Lucky Chance* at the Royal Court Theatre, 1984.

The beginning of the Behn revival: the Womens Playhouse production, directed by Jules Wright, with (from left to right) Alan Rickman, Harriet Walter, Denis Lawson, and Kathryn Pogson.

Christina Burton and the Womens Playhouse Theatre.

Observe that Lady dressed in the loose robe de Chambre *with her Neck and Breasts bare; how much Fire in her Eye! What a passionate Expression in her Motions! And how much Assurance in her Features! Observe what an Indignant Look she bestows on the President, who is telling her,* that none of her Sex has any Right to a Seat there. *How she throws her Eyes about, to see if she can find out any* one of the Assembly who inclines to take her Part. . . .

Fighting for recognition, her dissatisfied shade passes into history. Present-day feminists are right to keep a niche for her in their pantheon, and meanwhile her better work is once again finding its rightful place on the stage.

37. *The Rover*: engraving from an edition of 1735.

The scene illustrated is the life-threatening confrontation in the fifth act between the spurned Angellica and the rover, Willmore.

Collection of the late Montague Summers.

38. The young Princesses Mary and Anne with their parents,
the Duke and Duchess of York, by Sir Peter Lely and Gennari.

*Perhaps the execution leaves something to be desired, but the whole
has charm — as well as a scarcity value, for showing James's family
soon after the production of* Calisto *in 1675.*

H. M. the Queen.

ACT FIVE
Players and Playhouses

RESTORATION London supported two playhouses: the King's, finally established in Bridges Street, Covent Garden (and referred to here as Drury Lane), and the Duke's, first in Lincoln's Inn Fields and then in Dorset Gardens, off Fleet Street.

Perhaps it is logical, though, to start with the King's private theatres, since so many plays began their life there. In the history of court theatres (which continues right up to the destruction of Whitehall Palace in 1698, under William III) we catch the last glow of the great Jacobean and Carolean tradition that had drawn such magnificent work from Inigo Jones.

For an initial period, the converted 'Cockpit in Court' was used, adorned as early as November 1660 with 'Greene Manchester Bayes . . . and twenty faire gillt Branches' (candelabra). The dressing room was similarly hung, 'the walles being unfitt for the rich Cloathes', and provided with twenty 'chaires and stooles', a curtain to divide the sexes, and a 'looking glasse of twenty seaven Inches for the Women Comedians dressing themselves'.

Presently, in 1665, another theatre was built in Whitehall Palace, which Pepys, the following year, found 'very fine, yet bad for the voice, for hearing'. It was here that almost every popular play throughout the reign was presented, either before or after a showing in the public theatres. Pepys in 1666 was seeing an inferior cast in *Love in a Tub*, produced at the Duke's two years earlier. And it was here, in 1675, that the best-researched (thanks to Eleanor Boswell) court production of the period was staged — the *Calisto* written, with protestations of inadequacy, by the young John Crowne.

Calisto provides another *locus classicus* for Restoration theatre at its most typical. The leading parts were taken by the daughters of the Duke of York, Mary and Anne (both future Queens of England), with the Duke of Monmouth, the Duchess of Portsmouth's young sister, and others dancing *entrées*. Betterton, the finest actor at the Duke's theatre, and his wife produced. The River Thames, conveniently nymphified, appeared in the alluring guise of Moll Davis. Appropriately, the haughty Juno was played by the eldest daughter of Castlemaine by the King, and the conniving Mercury by young Sarah Jennings, later Duchess of Marlborough and Queen Anne's malicious confidante.

All were still in their teens except for Diana — the most crucial part of all, taken by Margaret Blagge, a former Maid of

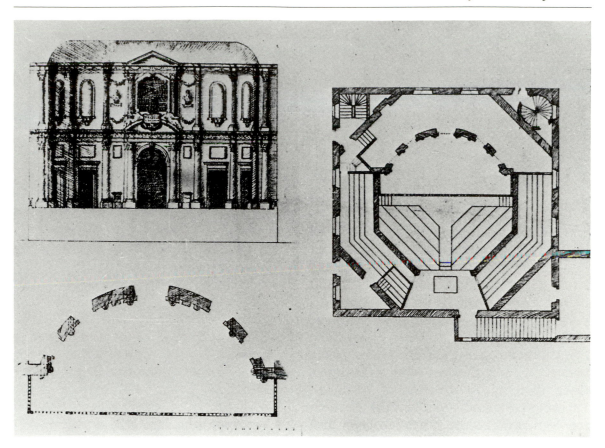

39. The Cockpit-in-Court: the designs of Inigo Jones and John Webb, 1631-32.

Not comparable in magnificence or longevity, but the closest England came to creating a court theatre equivalent to its great European counterparts. Charles must have greatly envied his cousin Louis XIV, who was rapidly developing his palace and grounds at Versailles as a centre of culture and courtly entertainment.

Worcester College, Oxford.

Honour who had been dragooned into it anyhow and spent all her time offstage sitting in a corner with her prayer book, so earning John Evelyn's special approval.

The whole show probably cost over £5000, relatively as much as a modern production designed to last a decade at Covent Garden. The theatre was specially redecorated (a new peacock and eagle made their appearance somewhere) and freshened with 600 yards of distemper.

New curtains were provided, 'of Blew Red and White in Breadths of Stuff'. And the costumes were magnificent: Diana appeared in 24 yards of gold brocade (worth half the Laureate's annual salary) and dozens of yards of gold and silver lace. America's dress incorporated '6000 swan's feathers of several colours', while Charles Hart (as Europe) wore skirts and sleeves

of silver tabby and longets of gold gawes

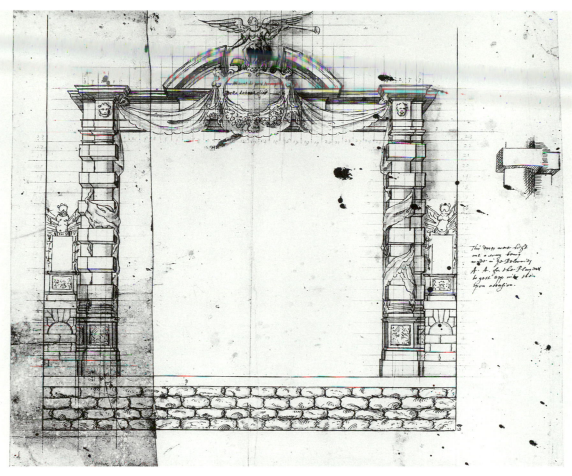

40. Probable design for the Hall Theatre, Whitehall Palace, by John Webb.

This sketch has been identified as Webb's design for the proscenium when Charles II's principal court theatre was reconstructed early in 1665. Note the figure of Fame blowing her trumpet. Splashes of scene-painters' distemper are still visible.

Chatsworth.

scollops round the wast and sey [sleeve-hole] *of silver tabby laced with gold fringe the bace sleeves and garters laced with gold Lace the body scollups and Hellmet adorned with Iewells and spangles the body sleeves and bace lined with deamoty the hellmet adorned with feathers and a paire of white taffeta drawers.*

Margaret Blagge borrowed jewels worth close on £20,000 — and lost one, which the Duke of York ended up paying for.

The words, of course, being only of secondary importance, Crowne's script is more of a credit to his diplomacy than to his dramatic inspiration. Pressed for time, he had to pick a mythological subject almost instantaneously; he chose well, with his all-female cast in mind, but

41. Thomas Killigrew, by William Sheppard.

The 'merry droll' and patentee of the first theatre in Drury Lane.

National Portrait Gallery, London.

not too wisely. Calisto, an attendant on the virginal Diana, was, in Ovid's legend, ravished by Jupiter — thus incurring a disgrace that inspired one of Rubens's finest paintings. But by judicious rewriting, the required Sunday-school respectability was achieved, and Crowne had to content himself with some elegant irony which did not go unappreciated. He thus preached a sermon on chastity to the most lecherous king in English history, and depicted him recognisably in the figure of Jupiter:

And since Your Rule such joy to all procures,
All should contribute what they can to Yours.

Some of course, contributed more than others. Nor could Charles have bettered Jupiter's statement of intent in Act III:

For I will be controul'd in no Amour;
My Love is arbitrary as my power.

Once again, and in the most magnificent setting, we have the same situation: a scene on stage echoing, depicting, parodying, a scene enacted in life by members of the audience.

*

When, at the beginning of his reign, Charles came to select patentees for the two commercial theatres, the choice was obvious. Only two major playwrights, Thomas Killigrew and Sir William Davenant — none of the authors so far mentioned, and few actors — formed a link with the theatre of the reign of Charles I. Both proved successful at moving with the times. Davenant, indeed, had been in management very recently,

maintaining various dramatic ventures even under the Commonwealth.

Killigrew (1612-83) had no management experience, but plenty of flair and rather better connections. He accompanied the King in his exile, even representing him as Resident in Venice despite almost total ignorance of Italian. When the Venetian Senate recognised Cromwell's government and 'Signor Chiligreo' was rudely dismissed, Charles did not forget him. Davenant was abler, but anyone who had temporised with Cromwell's regime, for whatever purpose, still caused some resentment.

In any case, Killigrew was a man after the King's heart. His jovially cynical humour, frequently directed at his master, was exactly what Charles wanted around him — in a more elegant form, it was what ensured that Rochester never left the court for long. Pepys first met him as part of the King's entourage on his triumphal return in 1660: 'Among others, Thom. Killigrew (a merry droll, but a gentleman of great esteem with the King) . . . told . . . many merry stories.' (That 'but' is astonishing: Samuel was soon to know his sovereign better.)

A mere six weeks later, on 9 July 1660, Killigrew had an order for a royal warrant granting himself and Davenant a monopoly — virtually essential when intending to run two quite large theatres for a limited audience. First a united company played at the Cockpit in Drury Lane; then in November the troupes split and Killigrew's, with the title of the King's Men, moved to a real-tennis court in Vere Street, Clare Market, off the Strand.

His agreement with Davenant included a division of the repertoire as well as the

42. Henry Harris as Cardinal Wolsey
in Shakespeare's *Henry VIII*: John Greenhill.

*An elegant and intelligent actor, Harris was esteemed
for his 'airiness' in comedy, and accordingly badgered
Davenant for vast salary increases and had to be
restrained by the King from deserting to Drury Lane.
Pepys testifies to the brilliance of his company and his
sense of fun, while affecting disapproval of some of his
activities: he belonged to a group who were found
dancing naked in the presence of Mother Bennet, the
procuress to whom Wycherley ironically dedicated*
The Plain-Dealer, *and her 'ladies'.*

Ashmolean Museum, Oxford.

cast — an economic necessity which, giving actors a monopoly of certain roles, deprived audiences of our modern pleasure and profit from comparing interpretations. This document, of course, throws interesting light on what they

expected to be popular. New works certainly appear from the outset, but Beaumont and Fletcher, plus the lesser Jacobean dramatists, are prominent. So are a handful of Shakespeare plays, but Killigrew lacked Davenant's contacts with Shakespeare (of which more presently) and seems to have underestimated his appeal; for he let Davenant have most of the masterpieces, including *Lear*, *Hamlet*, *Macbeth*, *Much Ado*, and *The Tempest*. No doubt he shirked the extra effort they involved, preferring the more predictable success of romantic comedies and lightweight dramas, but he must soon have realized his mistake. At the Duke's theatre, 'no succeeding Tragedy for several Years got more Reputation or Money to the Company' than *Hamlet*; *Twelfth Night* 'had mighty Success by its well Performance'; *Henry VIII* 'continued Acting fifteen days together', an almost unprecedented success.

Killigrew's plays convey quite a good idea of his cheerful, ebullient intelligence, if taken in small doses. But they never can be; even the best known, *The Parson's Wedding* (probably written in the 1640s) largely comprises reams of verbose waggery. Surely, his charm transfigured that prolixity when in conversation; but it does remain a mystery how any actor can have learnt (or spoken without asphyxiation), or any audience have sat through, such endless, rambling, profoundly undramatic sentences and speeches.

Yet the shrewdness and bite never wholly disappears. Consider Killigrew's one recorded contribution to state affairs, reported by Pepys on 8 December 1666:

There is a good, honest, able man that I could

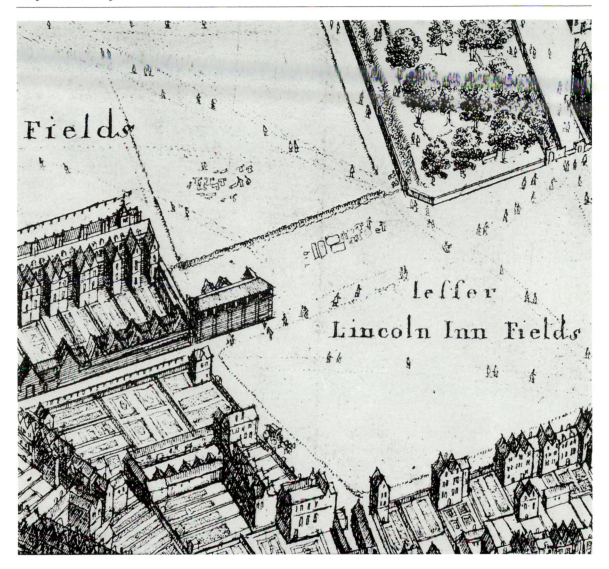

43. Prospect of Lincoln's Inn Fields: engraving by Wenceslaus Hollar, *c.* 1658.

This is a fine engraving, and is a section of a single sheet which Hollar prepared at this time to raise interest and patronage in a much larger map and survey of London. He was unfortunately still trying to secure the future of the project when much of his preparatory work was rendered obsolete by the Great Fire of London. Although Charles had granted him the title Scenographus Regius, he did little more cartography in London, the energy for this project being taken up by Ogilby and Morgan. This section clearly shows Lisle's tennis court in what is now Portugal Street, Lincoln's Inn Fields. Tudor and Jacobean tennis courts had no windows in the lower walls, but, as is clearly visible, here a row of windows ran round the top just below the eaves to light the interior. Davenant created his Duke's Playhouse in this building in 1661.

British Library.

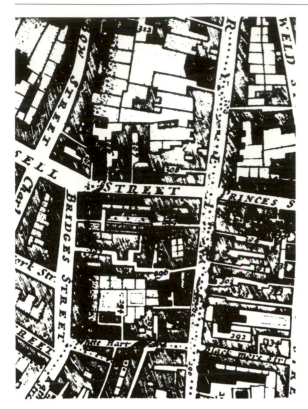

44. The first Drury Lane: a mapmaker's view.

This section of Morgan's map of London, although published in 1682, is believed to show the exterior of the first Drury Lane theatre. The rotunda (which Pepys complains of letting in rain) stands at the centre of the building — presumably over the pit.

Guildhall Library, London.

name, that if your Majesty would employ and command to see all things well executed, all things would soon be mended; and this is one Charles Stuart, who now spends his time in employing his lips about the Court, and hath no other employment. . . .

*

Beside Killigrew, Sir William Davenant (1606-68) and his plans for the Duke's

Men present a notable comparison in styles. Though genial, lively, and flexible of mind, he retained an old-fashioned integrity which contrasts with Killigrew's cheerful chicanery and increasing incompetence, punctuated by incessant pestering of his royal patron for lucrative sinecures.

By 1660, Davenant was nearing the end of a long, chequered career that was rather more dramatic than most plays. He was born in Oxford, son of a mayor who ran a tavern on the High and, it is reputed, entertained Shakespeare. According to that incorrigible gossip John Aubrey, Davenant implied that his mother had also entertained Shakespeare, suggesting an obvious source for his dramatic gifts. Like Killigrew, he too spent his early decades as a promising young courtier; though, typically, he managed to run more risks for the Crown while gaining less durable prestige.

His first play was produced as early as 1629. His work at this stage still inhabits the world of Jonson and Ford, but fresh and entertaining comedies like *News from Plymouth* (1635) and the spirited, acid verse of *The Just Italian* (1630) show unmistakable talent. To his dying day he was thought of as principally a playwright, as one Restoration reference proves. Early in life he lost his nose following an infection for which a 'black, handsome wench that lay in Asse-yard, Westminister' seems to have been responsible; so that, when Bayes comes on in *The Rehearsal* at Drury Lane with a patch over his nose, one naturally identifies him with the venerable anti-Cyrano at the rival theatre.

Davenant and his company moved in 1661 from their temporary theatre to another converted real-tennis court, in Lincoln's Inn Fields. Killigrew's new theatre in Bridges Sreet (corresponding to the modern Catherine Street, where the confusingly-named Theatre Royal, Drury Lane, stands to this day) was ready in 1663. These are the two playhouses through most of the period of Pepys's *Diary*. Pepys, indeed, was in on the second day at Bridges Street, and described it as being 'made with extraordinary good contrivance', except for narrow aisles and boxes that seemed too far away for audibility.

When Davenant died in 1668, the Duke's company was fully established. 'I was at his funerall', said Aubrey proudly. 'He had a coffin of Walnutt-tree; Sir John Denham sayd 'twas the finest coffin that ever he saw.' He was buried in Westminster Abbey, beneath an epitaph which a trifle ludicrously, recalled Ben Jonson's: 'O rare Sir Will. Davenant'.

Under his widow's direction, with his leading actor Thomas Betterton firmly in command, Davenant's old company moved in 1671 to a glamorous new theatre at Dorset Gardens, south of Fleet Street on the Thames, not far from where Wren's St Bride's was currently rising. (The Lord Mayor protested that the City's youth were already sufficiently corrupted with sensual pleasures; if the King made a witty retort, it is not preserved.) The charming river frontage, with its statues of the muses and the Duke's arms, appears in a number of prints. As for the interior, the engravings printed with *The Empress of Morocco*, one of its early successes, may be accurate; and a verse of D'Urfey's preserves an account of the auditorium after twenty years' dilapidation:

THE DUKE'S THEATRE.
Dorset Garden.

45. The new Duke's playhouse in Dorset Garden.

An engraving from the illustrated edition of Elkanah Settle's The Empress of Morocco. *This theatre, which opened in November 1671, may, like the Drury Lane of 1674, have been the work of Wren. Note, on the facade, the muses of Comedy and Tragedy flanking the arms of the Duke of York. The upper floors contained apartments, one being used by Betterton (Davenant had had one in the previous Duke's playhouse).*

Bristol Theatre Collection.

Each box with beauty crown'd,
And pictures deck the structure round;
Ben, Shakespear, and the learned rout,
With noses some, and some without.

Though some critics have imagined

Checks for the Theatre Dorset Gardens.

46. Admission tokens for the Duke's playhouse: a nineteenth-century engraving.

These were purchased at the door and then surrendered inside the auditorium.

Mander and Mitchenson Collection.

mutilated statues like the Sheldonian's at Oxford, presumably the new theatre simply boasted a portrait of the company's founder, who had died only three years before? From contemporary descriptions, we can recognise its layout as on familiar Victorian lines, with dress circle and upper circle as tiers of boxes, and a balcony above.

A few months later, the Duke's Men had the satisfaction of lending their own Lincoln's Inn Fields theatre to the King's company between the burning of Drury Lane in January 1672 and its reconstruction by Wren, the new theatre opening in March 1674. Even after the rebuilding, Drury Lane had a considerable inferiority complex. In his first Prologue in the new theatre, Dryden observes:

A Plain built House, after so long a stay,
Will send you half unsatisfi'd away; . . .
They, who are by your Favours wealthy made,
With mighty Sums may carry on the Trade;
We, broken Banquiers, half destroy'd by Fire,
With our small Stock to humble Roofs retire;
Pity our Loss, while you their Pomp admire.

Years of unrest followed, aggravated by Killigrew's mismanagement; nor were the political troubles during 1678-81, which included the departure of the Court to Oxford, a help to box-office receipts. When in 1682 the companies were reunited, it was virtually a takeover of Drury Lane by the Duke's Men. Most of the leading actors at the Lane retired and Killigrew died within the year, leaving Betterton head of the company.

In the same prologue, Dryden complains that home-grown dramas are being neglected in favour of 'Scenes, Machines and empty *Opera*' from 'Troops of famish'd Frenchmen' — a pleasing anticipation of the 'fasting Monsieur' that Dr Johnson translated from Juvenal in the following century. Davenant's commercial shrewdness had started this policy in his lifetime, some ten years earlier. As well as producing the Shakespeare plays that fitted contemporary taste, he did not hesitate to adapt the less promising pieces, as drastically as seemed necessary. *Macbeth* (1664) was made simultaneously popular and genteel to conform with current standards of poetic language and prosody:

Make haste, dark night,
And hide me in a smoke as black as hell,
That my keen steel see not the wound it makes,

47. Cross-section of a playhouse, by Sir Christopher Wren.

This is generally believed to be the second Drury Lane theatre, opened in 1674. As such, it is the only extant picture of this theatre before the many prints showing it after the Adam brothers' redecoration of 1775. It is, of course, a most important drawing since it is the first architect's design of a public theatre since the Inigo Jones drawings for the Cockpit in Drury Lane, c. 1616, reproduced on page 97. It presents no great surprises for us, and confirms our general understanding of the Restoration auditorium arrangement into a pit of benches surrounded by galleries and boxes. There is, however, no indication on this plan of a place for the orchestra. In The Empress of Morroco *illustration for the Duke's playhouse (page 77, above), the musicians appear to be housed centrally, above the proscenium arch. It is possible, although not confirmed by Wren's drawing, that they were so placed in this theatre.*

All Souls' College, Oxford.

Nor heav'n peep through the curtains of the dark,
To cry, Hold, hold!

Davenant also took *Measure for Measure* and *Much Ado* and amalgamated them. The result, *The Law Against Lovers* (1662), was, perhaps surprisingly, commercially unsuccessful, but nevertheless works well. Besides, the idea is entertaining in itself; cast-list entries like 'Benedick, brother to Angelo' begin to make one wonder if one is reading a play or an old *New Statesman* competition.

But most revealing, from the point of view of Restoration taste, is *The Tempest* (1667), Davenant's last work, in which he collaborated with Dryden. Shakespeare's magic, mysterious romance is carpentered into a thoroughly Restoration piece of work featuring two 'mad couples', none of whom have ever seen the opposite sex — a situation that stimulated Dryden to some of his most pleasing *jeux d'esprit*:

MIRANDA. *Shortly we may chance to see that thing,*
Which you have heard my Father call, a Man.

48. Angelo and Isabella in *Measure for Measure*.

Although some years later than the Restoration, this frontispiece to Nicholas Rowe's 1709 edition of Shakespeare suggests the relationship between the performers on their neutral forestage, backed by scenery which serves not as a scenic environment but as an apposite background to action.

DORINDA. *But what is that? For yet he never told me.*

MIRANDA. *I know no more than you: But I have heard*

My Father say, we Women were made for him.

DORINDA. *What, that he should eat us, Sister? . . .*

But pray, how does it come, that we two are

Not Brothers then, and have not Beards like him?

MIRANDA. *Now I confess you pose me.*

This is trivial, but so enchanting that one can almost forgive its origin as a parasite on a masterpiece. Equally delightful is the virginal Hippolito, who, having seen Dorinda, decides he would like all the women available. Indeed, he will fight for them, if only he knew what a sword was and could find one growing somewhere. It may not seem creditable to have turned *The Tempest* into a teenagers' version of *Marriage à-la-Mode*, but Sir Walter Scott's sneering description of the piece as a 'wild landscape converted into a formal parterre' infected with 'premature coquetry' and the germ of vice, judges it by standards we must try to suspend. It has a literacy and charm lacking in the crudely spectacular operatic versions — and in these days, before Purcell wrote or Monteverdi was performed, opera was identified in England with the crudest spectacle. Though the execution was substantially Dryden's, the ideas, as he admits, were Davenant's (including the creation of Hippolito).

*

Thomas Betterton (1635-1710) was not only the greatest actor of his age, and one of history's finest Hamlets: he was a man of exceptional integrity and modesty. What is more surprising, he gained the wholehearted respect and affection of his less principled colleagues and patrons. Where we find Hart bedding his orange-girl and accepting £100 under the counter from Killigrew's son in return for a new

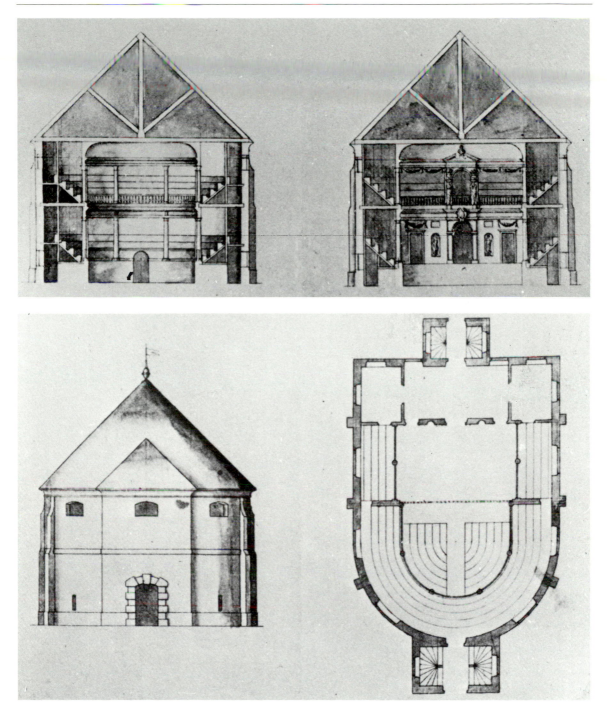

49. The Cockpit in Drury Lane.
Plans and elevations by Inigo Jones, c. 1616-18 (Worcester College, Oxford).

50. Thomas Betterton, after Sir Godfrey Kneller, *c.* 1690-1700.

A leading actor on the London stage for fifty years, and for half that time its undisputed king. 'I never heard a Line in Tragedy come from Betterton', wrote Colley Cibber, recalling his days as a young actor in Betterton's company, 'wherein my Judgement, my Ear, and my Imagination, were not fully satisfy'd.' He died in 1710, two days after an unforgettable farewell performance, and was buried in Westminster Abbey.

National Portrait Gallery, London.

contract, Betterton is only recorded as losing his temper when the youthful Colley Cibber wrecked a scene by his nervousness, and, on hearing he had no salary, crying 'Then put him down ten shillings a week, and forfeit him five.' Cibber remembered him gratefully for his gentle, helpful encouragement and his 'indirect reproofs', adding that 'He was naturally cheerful and had a very high confidence in Providence.'

Betterton's career with Davenant started young, probably just before the Restoration when Sir William's company was playing at the Cockpit. Betterton and Kynaston, in the initially all-male company, commonly appeared *en travesti*; but Betterton, lacking Kynaston's pretty face and far excelling him in genius, quickly graduated to mature leads, playing Hamlet, Sir Toby Belch, Mercutio, and Bosola in the 1660-61 season alone, as well as important roles in forgotten plays. On the stage, his grace and dignity transfigured natural disadvantages like his short limbs, big face, and rather portly figure — though that must have come in useful for *Henry VIII*, a part for which (like Hamlet) he was able to draw on Davenant's contact with Lowin, who had been instructed by Shakespeare himself.

One has the impression that he would not have seemed pompous or stilted, even today. Repeatedly there are references to his subtlety, how he lent truth and credibility to fustian, and how his intense concentration compelled attention and inspired solemnity in the pit's giddiest fantasticks.

Scarcely a new play at the Duke's appeared without him. Equally successful in modern comedy, he created the swash-buckling lead roles in the best comedies of Otway and Mrs Behn, and even Dorimant in *The Man of Mode*. (For a plain, plump man successfully to impersonate Rochester was an achievement indeed.) Betterton

51. Betterton as Hamlet.

Another engraving from Nicholas Rowe's 1709 edition of Shakespeare, this shows Betterton being surprised by the ghost in the closet scene. Betterton naturally wears contemporary clothes, although his stockings are suitably 'down-gyv'd'. Pursuing the logic of such an attitude to stage costume gives us a ghost wearing the armour of the previous generation. Betterton continued and established the piece of stage business (said to have been passed down from Burbage himself) whereby the chair is overturned as Hamlet rises in shock at his father's appearance.

survived into the age of Congreve, playing Valentine in *Love for Love* and Fainall in *The Way of the World* when he was over sixty.

Of one of his last Hamlets, *The Tatler* remarked: 'By the prevalent Power of proper Manner, Gesture and Voice, [he] appeared through the whole *Drama* a young man of great Expectation, Vivacity and Enterprize.' 'Could *how Betterton* spoke be as easily known as *what* he spoke', wrote Cibber, 'then you might see the Muse of *Shakespear* in her Triumph. . . . I never heard a Line in Tragedy come from *Betterton*, wherein my Judgment, my Ear, and my Imagination, were not fully satisfy'd.'

*

Though Betterton's wife, one of the first women on the London stage and his original Ophelia, remained a leading lady for fifty years, rather more of the important roles went to Elizabeth Barry (1658-1713). Now the partnership between Betterton and Mrs Barry must, in personal terms, be accounted one of the most extraordinary in British theatre history. Even the private lives of Sir Johnston Forbes-Robertson and Mrs Patrick Campbell were not more widely contrasted.

After an unpromising beginning, at the age of fifteen, Mrs Barry, as we have seen, was taken in hand by Rochester. When preparing her for her first part, he put her through twelve dress rehearsals alone. Like Professor Higgins, he undertook to make a success out of the least hopeful material — for she could neither speak, nor act, nor dance (and, like Betterton, never did the last of these successfully).

One cannot tell whether Rochester saw glimmers of a great genius in her, or whether he simply set out to make her competent, knowing that practice and opportunity can usually produce, from nothing, talent that appears to deserve its success.

Certainly her personality was admirably suited to the theatre; and her looks were noble and voluptuous. Few in the audience remained unmoved by her stage persona; fewer still were deceived by it. One judgement called her 'the finest person in the world upon the stage, and the ugliest woman off on't.' Her immorality excited remark even in her own licentious period. She did not bother to pretend fidelity to the patron who started her career, let alone the playwright who brought it so much success.

In fact, the parts Otway wrote for her are the best sources we have for her particular style of pathos — a trifle dated, we may feel. The pathos will be redoubled if we recognise Otway's transparent fantasy in casting her, time and time again, as an innocent, pure, and intensely loyal woman:

And may no fatal minute ever part us,
Till, reverend grown, for age and love, we go
Down to one Grave, as our last bed, together,
There sleep in peace till an eternal morning.

Put beside this the heart-rending letters that he almost certainly addressed to her:

Since the first Day I saw you, I have hardly enjoy'd one Hour of perfect Quiet. . . . I appeal to yourself for Justice, if through the whole Actions of my Life I have done any one thing that might not let you see how absolute your

Authority was over me. . . . You never were belov'd or courted by a Creature *that had a* nobler *or* juster *Pretence to your* Heart, *than the* Unfortunate *and (even at this time)* Weeping OTWAY.

Rochester fared little better; his brilliant letters chronicle the affair from radiant brilliance to its sullen, indifferent extinction, whereas Otway's only record its final convulsions, deliberately prologued by the Barry herself: 'a *kind Look*, and after it a *cruel Denial*.' Yet she did become one of the great tragediennes, even comediennes, of the age; her *dégagé* sex-appeal perfectly fitted the heroines of Mrs Behn and Ravenscroft, being, 'in free Comedy . . . alert, easy, and genteel'.

But she seems to have excelled in tragedy, and the tributes are warm, if rather lacking in individuality. Her 'softness'; the real tears that she always shed, and drew from the audience, on 'O poor Castalio!' in Otway's *The Orphan*; her grandeur as Queen Elizabeth in *The Unhappy Favourite*, or *The Earl of Essex*, for which James II's queen lent her coronation robes; and her ability, while remaining 'impetuous and terrible', to 'pour out the Sentiment with an enchanting Harmony': all these attributes are impressive, without quite convincing us — as Betterton, Nell Gwyn, and the Mountforts do — that we have missed something we would truly have enjoyed.

She survived Otway's wretched death by nearly thirty prosperous years — which even included Congreve premieres, for irresistible Mrs Frail and treacherous Mrs Marwood might have been written expressly to exploit both sides of her personality. Not inaptly, her death in 1713

is said to have followed a bite from a rabid lapdog.

❉

Comic leads at the Duke's were in the broad and capable hands of James Nokes and Cave Underhill. Underhill, an irresistibly lugubrious portrayer of rustic dullness, was also famous for 'roaring in coffee-houses' — where, it is recorded,

52. Cave Underhill.

This portrait of the actor as Obadiah in Sir Robert Howard's The Committee; or, The Faithful Irishman *(1662) indicates a combination of mournfulness and wit which must have had a lot in common with George Robey.*

Mary Evans Picture Library.

53. Tony Leigh as the Spanish Fryar:
Sir Godfrey Kneller, 1689.

*This subtly comic portrait of Leigh's performance
in Dryden's comedy of 1680 (whose character largely
disappears in engravings) is said to have been
'extremely like'.*

National Portrait Gallery, London.

his favourite tipple was Bristol Milk. Inevitably, he was the Gravedigger to Betterton's Hamlet, and this was how Anthony Aston saw him:

His Nose was flattish and short, and his Upper Lip very long and thick, with a wide Mouth and short Chin, a churlish Voice, and awkward Action, leaping often up with both Legs at a Time, when he conceived any Thing waggish, and afterwards hugging himself at the Thought.

Davenant said he was the truest comedian in the company. Nokes's *forte*, on the other hand, was hopeless silliness — 'piteous, they made a perfect pair'.

Typical of Nokes's parts was Jorden (M. Jourdain) in Ravenscroft's enormously successful adaptation of the *Bourgeois Gentilhomme*. As Sir Martin Mar-All, stupidly wrecking all the plots made on his behalf and always realising too late, his comical contrition convulsed the house. In Otway's *Caius Marius*, that wholesale theft from *Romeo and Juliet* in which someone even says 'O Marius, Marius! wherefore art thou Marius?', his performance in drag gave him the name Nurse Nokes for life.

His part of the Frenchified fop in Wycherley's *The Gentleman Dancing Master* contains extravagant praise of himself at the expense of Angel, who was probably in the same play. (Sheridan worked the trick a century later, when Thomas King, as Puff in *The Critic*, had the satisfaction of saying 'It is not in the power of language to do justice to Mr King!') When Nokes died in 1696, it is pleasant to record that he left an estate of over £1500, including a sword given him by the Duke of Monmouth.

Almost as popular as these two giants was Tony Leigh (or Lee), most famous for his Antonio, the vicious caricature of Shaftesbury in *Venice Preserv'd*. Other roles were astonishingly varied — quicksilver servants like Scapin, Mercury, and Scaramouch, camp old eccentrics like Pandarus and Sir Jolly Jumble, Dryden's deliciously Falstaffian Spanish Fryar ('Never was such a Ton of Devotion seen'), and gruff Sir William (rather like an unsympathetic Sir Anthony Absolute) in *The Squire of Alsatia*. When he acted with Nokes, we are told that 'they returned the Ball so dextrously upon one another, that every Scene between them, seem'd but one continued Rest of Excellence'.

All in all, Davenant chose his players shrewdly and built a company strong enough to flatter the most inconsequential plays. If we seek to explain the wild success of an amiable farrago such as Shadwell's *Epsom Wells* (1672), we need look no further than the cast: Nokes, Underhill and Angel, Betterton and his wife, all in brilliantly characteristic roles, with one Mrs Johnson as the young female lead Carolina, who 'danced a Jigg so Charming well, Love's power in a little time after Coerc'd her to Dance more Charming else-where'. Similarly, the moment in *The Old Bachelor* which brought together the four most beautiful women on the English stage (Barry, Bracegirdle, Bowman, and Mountfort) moved the audience to prolonged applause in a *frisson* of delight.

*

Partly because we have the memoirs of John Downes, the prompter at the Duke's, partly because the Duke's actors were younger and survived into a better-documented period, we know more about their company than the King's. Charles Hart, Michael Mohun, and several of their colleagues had actually been performing in the 1640s. Hart (who was the grandson of Shakespeare's sister Joan) was a popular, flamboyant performer in both tragedy and comedy — who, if not as thoughtful as Betterton, must have had great power and charm. Almost all of Dryden's romantic heroes were written for

him, as well as Wycherley's Horner and Manly. A member of the court said he could have taught grace of deportment to any prince in Europe.

Mohun, as befitted his name's pronunciation, was generally regarded as the second light, though he seems to have been more intelligent and versatile. The King said after one play that he had shone like the sun, and Hart like the moon. Rochester, too, preferred him, which may not have been just perverseness. He obviously did well, and had the handsomest house in Russell Street.

As well as playing second leads like Ventidius to Hart's Antony in *All for Love*, he was successful as Volpone to Hart's Mosca, and in character roles like the cuckold Pinchwife. Twenty-five years after their deaths, *The Tatler* declared, in a piece usually attributed to Steele: 'My old Friends, *Hart* and *Mohun*; the one by his natural and proper Force, the other by his great Skill and Art; never failed to send me Home full of such Ideas as affected my Behaviour, and made me insensibly more courteous and humane to my Friends and Acquaintance.' (There is an anomaly here, previously, I think, unrecognised: Steele cannot here be speaking for himself, as both actors died when he was a boy. But it does serve to show how legendary the partnership was.)

Edward Kynaston was younger and survived to act in the early Congreve performances. At the Lane, he successfully graduated from female parts to romantic heroes without loss of grace. Something of a matinee idol before his time, he had fashionable ladies vying to take him for a drive in full costume after performances. But on one occasion he walked alone: after aping Sir Charles Sedley's person and dress in a play by the Duke of Newcastle, he even took a stroll round St James's Park in character. Sedley had him so soundly thrashed that he couldn't act for a week. (Attempting to dignify his revenge with a sense of style and dramatic invention, he instructed his thugs to pretend they were after the real Sedley.)

*

With the company's leading lady, we reach well-trodden ground. Here is a character-sketch by Madame de Sévigné, written in 1675, telling how Nell Gwyn supplanted the French Duchess of Portsmouth in the King's affections:

[*Kéroualle*] *n'a été trompée sur rien; elle avoit envie d'être la maîtresse du roi, elle l'est. . . . Elle amasse des trésors, et se fait redouter et respecter de qui elle peut. Mais elle n'avoit pas prévu de trouver en son chemin une jeune comédienne dont le roi est ensorcelé. . . . La comédienne est aussi fière que la duchesse de Portsmouth; elle la morgue* [insults], *elle lui fait la grimace, elle l'attaque, et lui dérobe souvent le roi; elle se vante de ses préférences: elle est jeune, folle, hardie, débauchée, et plaisante.*

Young, crazy, cheeky, debauched, entertaining: Nell Gwyn has seldom been better described. At fourteen or so, she was working 'front of house' at Drury Lane; at sixteen she was playing the lead; at eighteen she became the King's mistress; at twenty she retired. Her ascendancy was brief but brilliant. Petite, voluptuous, deliciously mischievous on and off the stage, she was a gift to comic roles and

was much missed when she took her incorrigible high spirits away to the grander auditoria of the court. Beauty apart, she suited the cynical, irreverent Charles perfectly: who else would have referred to James II as 'dismal Jimmy'?

Her efforts in tragedy were pretty terrible — Pepys saw her in a 'great and serious part' by Dryden and reckoned she did it 'most basely' — but her romantic ardour must have had some effect when she played *The Conquest of Granada* opposite her former lover, Charles Hart. After another intense role in Dryden's *Tyrannick Love*, which required her to die in the last act, she was allowed a comic epilogue which involved her shouting at the bearers who came to take her off: 'Hold, are you mad? You damn'd confounded Dog, / I am to rise, and speak the Epilogue.' Tragedy as light entertainment again.

Of her Celia in the favourite Drury Lane play, Beaumont and Fletcher's *Humorous Lieutenant*, Pepys remarked on 23 January 1667 that she acted this 'great part . . . very fine', adding, rather startlingly, 'I kissed her, and so did my wife.' Six weeks later, after seeing her in Dryden's *Secret Love*, his admiration burst its banks: 'So great performance of a comical part was never, I believe, in the world before.'

This inspired Nell's Victorian biographer, Peter Cunningham, to one of his most brilliantly imaginative pages, describing her performance, disguised as a handsome young man to outwit her lover (again the *travesti*), 'dressed to the admiration of Etherege and Sedley, scanned from head to foot with much surprise by Mr Pepys and Sir William Penn, viewed with other feelings by Lord Buckhurst on

54. The Introduction of Pepys to Nell Gwyn: Augustus Egg, 1850.

'And Knipp took us all in, and brought us to Nelly, a most pretty woman, who acted the part of Coelia to-day very fine, and did it pretty well: I kissed her, and so did my wife; and a mighty pretty soul she is'
(Pepys's Diary, 23 January 1667).

Museum of New Mexico.

one side of the house, and the King himself on the other.' That is Restoration theatre in a nutshell: a drama enacted in public, while an actress on stage guys exactly the same drama dressed as a man.

Nell retired, probably in 1671, to her house in Pall Mall (of which she claimed the freehold, on the grounds that the King had always had hers) and its silver bed with an exquisitely appropriate decoration of crowns and cupids — not to mention Jacob Hall dancing on his rope. Of the fondness she and Charles felt for each other there can be no doubt, though it was convenient that Charles the Third, as she called him (Hart and Buckhurst being the first two), combined the maximum of affection, even perhaps of physical endowment, with the most exalted rank.

The same irreverent wit that had, with gratifying results, inserted a laxative into Moll Davis's supper just before the latter's night with the King, now sent up the Duchess of Portsmouth for going into black whenever a death occurred in the French royal family. When she deflated Louise's snobbery, the King was on her side; and the English people agreed with him. One should not undervalue the famous story told of Parliament's meeting in Oxford during the Papist scare, when Nelly's coach, mistaken for Louise's, was furiously attacked until she put her head out and cried, 'Pray, good people, be civil; I am the *Protestant* whore.'

Mary Knep, Nelly's colleague and great friend, flits vivaciously through the pages of Pepys, who found her a sparkling source of gossip and an invaluable *entrée* backstage. His accounts of their music parties together are a piquant indication of the intimacy of Restoration society; how many modern actresses spend their evenings singing duets with promising young civil servants? Though she more or less resisted Pepys's advances, she may have yielded to those of Sedley, who probably wrote 'To Celia' with her in mind.

Opposite Mary Knep, as ingénue, was the baby-faced Elizabeth Boutell, who played at least three of Wycherley's heroines (including the Country Wife herself) and, very surprisingly, created Cleopatra in Dryden's *All for Love*, as well as his version of St Catherine as a steely, disputatious virgin.

Of the comics, John Lacey and Joe Haynes were the greatest. Lacey became

immortal for his Bayes in *The Rehearsal*, a performance in which he imitated Dryden so minutely that one is surprised the poet ever forgave him. 'As this Age never had, so the *next* never will have, his *Equal*, at least not his *Superiour*', says Langbaine, adding that Charles II kept a triple portrait of him at Windsor.

But Haynes was the greater character off-stage. Later anecdotists delighted in outrageous additions to the corpus of Haynes tales, though an actor who recited his own epilogues dressed as a ghost or riding a donkey hardly needed the embroidery of fiction. During James II's temporary imposition of Catholic *mores*, he is variously reported to have justified a raree-show of the Pope under the pretext that 'he shew'd him to be a fine, comely old Gentleman, as he was; not with Seven Heads, and ten Horns as the *Scotch* Parsons describe him', and to have claimed a personal vision of the Virgin Mary crying 'Arise, Joe!' ('She would have said *Joseph*', remarked Lord Sunderland, 'if it had been only out of respect to her husband.') He narrowly escaped a stay in the Bastille for impersonating an English peer, and deserved as bad for tricking £20 out of the Bishop of Ely. What this madcap made of great comic roles like Wycherley's Sparkish we can only guess.

*

The amalgamation of the companies in 1682 drove most of the older actors like Hart and Mohun from the stage. Of the coming generation, the best loved was Anne Bracegirdle, who inspired in the new playwright, Congreve, a devotion that brought her some of the greatest

55. John Lacy, by John Michael Wright, *c.* 1668-70.

This is the famous triple portrait commissioned by Charles II and now at Windsor Castle. The roles depicted here have not yet been clearly identified, but are most probably Sauny the Scot, in Lacy's own adaptation of The Taming of the Shrew, *and Scruple in John Wilson's* The Cheats, *scowling at each other across the scornfully Pepysian countenance of Lacy as a contemporary beau, probably Monsieur Device in the Duke of Newcastle's* The Country Captain.

H. M. the Queen.

56. Ann Bracegirdle.

The credentials of this little portrait are less than impressive, but it is the only one which conveys some of this actress's beauty and charm.

Victoria and Albert Museum, London.

female parts of the period, including Millamant. By contrast with Mrs Barry, who (according to one account) nearly killed her on stage one night, she had a reputation for purity that at times seems almost frigid. 'Wou'd she cou'd make of me a Saint, or I of her a Sinner!' wrote Congreve.

Presented with some fine porcelain by the Earl of Burlington, she promptly readdressed it to his wife, who was naturally thrilled by his adoring generosity. Yet one is greatly impressed by the four noble gentlemen who, disinterestedly, sent her 800 guineas 'with Encomiums on her Virtue', a present she presumably kept. Rather than any exceptional beauty, it seems to have been the 'Glow of Health and Chearfulness' in her 'fresh blushy Complexion', not to mention the 'involuntary Flushing in her Breast, Neck and Face . . . whenever she exerted herself' which ensured that 'few Spectators that were not past it, could behold her without Desire'. Aston adds that she never made an exit 'but that she left the Audience in an Imitation of her pleasant Countenance'.

Her leading man at the beginning of her career — his was destined to be short — was William Mountfort. The company's brightest hope in the 1680s and early 1690s, he left his mark on an extraordinary variety of roles — most of all, perhaps, those of refined comedy, if possible with a touch of romance. Yet characters like Sir Courtly Nice drew from him the true actor's gift of impersonation and submergence of self, new-minting his lines as if from his own thoughts, delivering wit apparently extempore 'to the highest Delight of his Auditors'. His excellence in tragedy encompassed 'the Great, the Tender, the Penitent, the Despairing, the Transported, and the Amiable, in the highest Perfection'. Tall, fair, and strikingly handsome, he was enormously popular (in spite of what seems to have been a close friendship with the hated Judge Jeffreys). His plays include some pleasant comedies as well as pot-boilers like a largely farcical rewrite of *Doctor Faustus*.

Susanna, his wife, was a distinguished comedienne in her own right, who sub-

57. Joe Haines, 1697.

This engraving shows the actor speaking the epilogue to The Unhappy Kindness, *one of Tom Brown's comedies, from the back of an ass. Note the ass's full-bottomed wig, which makes its human identification clear enough. The print is undated, and may be later than the incident, but it gives a rare (if somewhat architecturally confusing) glimpse into a playhouse of the period.*

Bristol Theatre Collection.

sequently married Jack Verbruggen, the first Mirabell in *The Way of the World*. Her forte was affected comedy, and Cibber has left us a minute description of her Melantha in *Marriage à-la-Mode*, throwing herself vocally and physically into deliciously impossible flights of whimsy. She also made the most of Berinthia in Vanbrugh's *The Relapse* (1696) — a character notable, under the offer of rape, for the quietest protest ever seen on the stage.

But we must return to Mountfort himself. This gifted and agreeable actor, who seems to have been largely forgotten except by theatrical scholars, would undoubtedly have matured into a figure of major importance — but for an early death which puts into perspective all those light-hearted tales of actresses' affairs with the nobility.

One Captain Hill, a lad of twenty, and Lord Mohun, a fifteen-year-old spark,

58 (left). Edward Kynaston: a nineteenth-century engraving after Sir Peter Lely.

Despite its likeness to a Murillo maiden or a sub-Raphaelite St. John, this is the only likeness we have.

59 (right). Charles, Baron Mohun, by Sir Godfrey Kneller, *c.* 1707.

The aristocratic accomplice in the attempted rape of Mrs Bracegirdle and murder of Mountfort.

Victoria and Albert Museum, London (left), and National Portrait Gallery (right).

'such as come drunk and screaming into a Play-House' tried and failed to abduct Mrs Bracegirdle. Having failed, they fixed their hatred on Mountfort, whose tenderness towards her on stage convinced them he must be her lover. (This need not have been true: Cibber reminds us that he acted 'the most affecting Lover within my Memory'.) On 9 December 1692 they encountered him on his way home from the theatre. Before he had time to defend himself, Captain Hill's sword had him through his stomach to a depth of twenty inches. He died a few hours later. The Captain escaped and was subsequently pardoned following the Duke of Marlborough's intervention.

Just a few weeks later, Congreve's first play went into rehearsal. In style, range, and relationship with the audience, this comedy moved into an entirely different world, but without the leading young actor who would have given it so much. The character parts in *The Double Dealer* would have been conceived very differently. He and Mrs Bracegirdle would have been still together to play the leads in *The Way of the World* and *Love for Love* (Mountfort would, with some regret, have allowed Bowman to play Tattle). And those two rather stolid roles, Mirabell and Valentine, would have gained an extra sparkle in the writing which is now lost to us for good.

Epilogue

60. James II, by Ann Killigrew, 1685.

'The new regime' painted by Thomas Killigrew's great-niece, shortly after James's accession in February 1685 and just before the young artist's death.

H. M. the Queen.

A FEW WEEKS before his death, Dryden wrote a sour epitaph for the seventeenth century in the finale of his 'Secular Masque':

All, all, of a piece throughout;
Thy Chase had a Beast in View;
Thy Wars brought nothing about;
Thy Lovers were all untrue.
'Tis well an Old Age is out,
And time to begin a New.

What was positively the last appearance of the King, of Nelly and many of the other characters in this book, was memorably, if damningly, reviewed by John Evelyn on 4 February 1685:

I am never to forget the unexpressable luxury and prophanesse, gaming and all dissolution, and as it were total forgetfullnesse of God (it being Sunday Evening), which this day sennight I was witnesse of; the King, sitting and toying with his Concubines, Portsmouth, Cleaveland, and Mazarine, etc., a French boy singing love songs, in that glorious Gallery. . . .

Six days after, as Evelyn continues, all was in the dust. On Charles II's lips, as he died, was a perfect expression of his wit, courtesy, and fundamental contempt for both life and death: 'I have been a most unconscionable time a-dying, but I hope that you will excuse it.' Even at the last, especially at the last, his dramatic instinct did not desert him. But then, as Tony Leigh is made to say in Tom Brown's *Letters*, 'Every Comedian ought to die with a Jest in his Mouth to preserve his Memory; for if he makes not the Audience Laugh as he goes off the Stage, he forfeits his Character.'

61. William III in triumph, escorted by Flora and Britannia:
Sir Godfrey Kneller, 1697.

According to Lucyle Hook (in Theatre Notebook, *XV, p. 129), the two
ladies in the bottom right of the picture are almost certainly Mrs Barry
(an identification confirmed by Horace Walpole) and Mrs Bracegirdle.*

H. M. the Queen.